ENTRANCE TO THE MAGICAL QABALAH

Melita Denning & Osbourne Phillips

THOTH PUBLICATIONS

First published 1997

Copyright © Denning & Phillips 1997

All rights reserved. No reproduction, copy or transmission of
this publication may be made without written permission.
No paragraph of this publication may be reproduced, copied or
transmitted save with written permission or in accordance with
the provision of the Copyright Act 1956 (as amended).
Any person who does any unauthorised act in relation to this
publication may be liable to criminal prosecution and civil
claims for damages.

The Moral Rights of the Authors have been asserted.

A CIP catalogue record for this book is available from the
British Library.

Cover design by Paul Hemstock

Printed and bound in Great Britain

Published by Thoth Publications
98 Ashby Road, Loughborough, LE11 3AF

ISBN 1 870450 35 3

Melita Denning passed within the veil
of the Great Mother on 23 March 1997
and so into the starry embrace of the beloved.

This book is filled with her light
and brings you her joyful greeting,
her companionship and her blessing.

CONTENTS

Part 1

THE FUNDAMENTALS

		page
1.	The Qabalah and the Zohar — a first word	9
2.	The Four Worlds and the dynamic archetypes	12
3.	The contribution of the Hermetic Corpus	20
4.	Traditions continued in the Zohar	25
5.	The Ten Sephiroth	35
6.	Binah and the seven planetary powers	41
7.	The Three Columns	46
8.	The Words of Power	52

Part 2

THE WORLDS OF THE FALLIBLE AND THE NATURE OF MAN

9.	The Qlippoth	61
10.	Humankind, earthly and archetypal	68
11.	The powers within us	74
12.	Heavens, hells and the soul	83
13.	Sons of the Most High	94

Part 3

THE PATHS AND THE WAY OF RETURN

14. The Ascent of the Tree   104

Part 4

CORRESPONDENCES

Table 1 ——	The ten Sephiroth	127
Table 2 ——	Sephirothic Divine Names	127
Table 3 ——	Planetary colours and metals	128
Table 4 ——	The Heavens of Assiah	128
Table 5 ——	The seven Heavens of Yetzirah	129
Table 6 ——	The seven Hells	129
Table 7 ——	The seven Palaces in Briah	129
Table 8 ——	The sephirothic choras of angels	130
Table 9(a) —	The Hebrew alphabet	130
Table 9(b) —	Influences on the alphabetic Paths	131
Table 10 ——	Archangels of the 32 Paths	132
Table 11 ——	Angels of the alphabetic Paths	133
Table 12 ——	Incenses, perfumes, botanical symbols	134
Table 13 ——	Gemstones and other minerals	135

Notes On The Correspondences   *137*

Bibliography   *165*

Part 1
THE FUNDAMENTALS

CHAPTER 1
THE QABALAH AND THE ZOHAR — A FIRST WORD

What the Qabalah is

The Qabalah is a master plan to open up understanding and to assist and clarify thought. Directly and indirectly (for it has many derivatives) it has given guidance and stimulation to major thinkers and writers in the past and present centuries in the fields of philosophy and psychology, religion and magic. The most illustrious minds of ancient and more recent times have helped to build the totality of Qabalistic knowledge and to interpret it, with the result that the student of this present age, equipped with a share of that knowledge, can embark upon his own programme of research, not in obscurity, but standing as it were upon the shoulders of those great ones of past and present.

This unparalleled instrument has been titled the Holy Qabalah, the Mystical Qabalah, and to us it is in addition the Magical Qabalah.

Besides all these aspects, it has also a profound psychological significance which, likewise, is relevant to the present work. For the student of magic, whether as practitioner or as theorist, needs as wide an understanding as possible of the scope of Qabalah; while the psychic, the prophet, the healer and the interpreter of dreams will be enabled to give their work greater focus and direction with this background knowledge of the spheres which they explore.

Aleister Crowley described the Qabalah as a filing system, in which we can store, accessibly and intelligibly, all the knowledge we gain. It is indeed such a system, but it is much more than that. The Qabalah gives to the student what is perhaps the most important element in all knowing and reasoning: **keys to the relationship of any one portion of our knowledge to the rest.**

Concerning the Zohar

One of the great sources of Qabalistic knowledge is the mediaeval Hebrew compilation known as the Zohar. A disputed authorship has been claimed for it, that of Moses of Leon who died in 1305.

Certainly he played an important part in its history, and from our point of view there is little need to regret the impossibility of probing further. Every original thinker is inevitably formed by his background and by his teachers. On the other hand, every paraphraser or translator inevitably colours his work with his own spirit as well as that of the material upon which he works. In any case, we may be immensely thankful to the memory of Moses of Leon if he did no more than to save this wonderful body of mystical literature from a probable oblivion.

The background of the Zohar and its compiler is the Jewish community in mediaeval Spain. In that brief and unequalled culture, Jewish, Christian and Islamic thinkers were free to exchange thoughts and to build new structures of philosophy, in the ambience of their own religious traditions and of the writings of the great philosophers of Greece. A tolerant and genial atmosphere prevailed until the more rigid elements in each party took fright, and the terrors of the Inquisition completed the ruin. But all the traditions involved had been lastingly influenced by that period of interchange.

The Zohar — a library

The Zohar, like the Bible, is not a book but a library. In its various parts, no matter how they may have been revised or collated, there can be perceived the underlying work of many minds.

Some parts are more Platonist in inclination, some more Aristotelian; some are emanationist in their view of the origin of things, some uncompromisingly creationist; some purely monistic, some virtually dualistic. Different portions are narrative, moralistic, meditative or purely poetic.

We can find in the Zohar Babylonian, Persian and later influences. There are even rare traces of yogic or Taoist concepts: not an impossible incidence, since other aspects of Taoist teaching had earlier appeared in the work of the great Arab physician and philosopher Avicenna (980—1037 A.D.)

A study of the Zohar at first hand is not needed by every magical student, but those who wish to undertake it are likely to find it fascinating. Anyone who seeks to gain this direct knowledge of it should, to begin with, take one volume at a time and read it through attentively. Then, as in every other great work, topics of particular interest can be chosen and traced as they recur in different contexts; ample notes should be made, and the matter related to other areas of knowledge. To do this increases the understanding of the text and also helps memory.

From time to time over the years this operation may be repeated. The student's perspective will change, and his recognition of interrelated passages will become keener. Certainly it is true that not all the Zohar is essential to Qabalah, and — for the magical student in particular — not the whole of Qabalah is comprised in the Zohar. Nevertheless, the Zohar remains a foundation work, and an extensive field for reflection and research.

CHAPTER 2
THE FOUR WORLDS AND THE DYNAMIC ARCHETYPES

The Four Worlds of the Qabalah

In the universe of the Qabalah are distinguished four "Worlds", which signify "levels of existence". Identified by their Hebrew names, these are *Atziluth* the world of the divine; *Briah* the world of mind; *Yetzirah* the astral world of imagery and emotion; and *Assiah* the world of matter.

Sometimes these four levels of existence are shown diagrammatically as horizontal layers in descending order: this is useful to remind the student to distinguish the functions of each of these levels apart from the others. As a fact, the functions of the four Worlds interpenetrate considerably, both in the outer cosmos and in our own being; but for that very reason care is needed not to confuse them in thought or in practical working.

Diagram and reality

In training oneself for magical work it is generally necessary to simplify for the time being one's view of a subject, so as to give it tautness and clarity in the understanding. However, having achieved this one must not take the diagram — even one's own mental diagram — for the reality. This distinction is particularly vital in regard to the Qabalah, for here the complex interaction of living forces is in question. In ourselves, for example, the three-way play of physical, emotional and intellectual activity is more easily observed than analysed, while few who accept the existence of the divine, the numinous, would dare set a limit to its levels of possible influence. Equally, if we look to astronomy, to space physics, to researches in radiation or in subatomic physics, it is evident that in itself the World of Assiah comprises infinite gradations from the densest to the most subtle.

An important example of the difference in function among the four Qabalistic Worlds can be given with reference to the nature and development of the gods. To begin with however, something must be said to introduce the archetypes.

A philosophic concept evolves: Plato and the "Ideas"

The great philosopher Plato (born about 428/7 B.C.) introduced into his theory of knowledge the concept of the "Forms" or "Ideas", the latter being the more renowned of his terms for them . Plato's references to them show them to be entirely spiritual, generated by the One, and — in the dialogue *Phaedo* — to subsist in a transcendent mode of existence which is also the primal state of the souls unborn.

Plato however was neither conforming to, nor assailing, any existing system. He was freely exploring his own world of thought, passing from topic to topic. Sometimes he developed a concept, sometimes he went back and revised an opinion or a mode of expression. To those who are looking for a system therefore his work, extensive though it is, shows gaps and omissions. His concept of the Ideas soon raised controversy and the term passed out of favour in the philosophic world. The perception itself, however, was not lost. Five hundred years later we find it newly expounded under a different name: the *archetypes*.

Philo of Alexandria

We owe our first meeting with the term "archetype" to Philo of Alexandria, a Jewish philosopher of the first century A.D. whose life's work it was to show the compatibility of Greek philosophy with a religious acceptance of the Old Testament.

He employed the term "archetype" to denote the spiritual principles of phenomena both animate and inanimate, which must exist in the Divine Mind to give those phenomena the possibility of real being. The use of the term "archetypes" thus indicates not only the existence but the relevance of the Divine Mind as their source, whereas the "Ideas" of Plato and the "emanations" of other writers presume only a supreme First Cause not necessarily possessing the attribute of conscious life which is associated with deity.

Philo and his students may not have been the only users of the term "archetype", for an outstanding occurrence of it appears in the third century, in a context which shows no relationship to Philo's work or beliefs. This is in the *Poimandres*, an important text of the *Corpus Hermeticum*, and a further account of it is given below.

Augustine of Hippo

The term "archetype" was again notably taken up in the fifth century by another great thinker of North Africa, St. Augustine of Hippo who was educated at Carthage. His theological and mystical writings as a Christian after his conversion from Manichaeism and Neoplatonism gained and retained a wide popularity in the western world. Of his Christian readers, those who were themselves of a mystical turn of mind welcomed particularly, for their own use, the vocabulary and the organised system which he presented.

Carl G. Jung

Since the time of Augustine, the most important development in our understanding of the archetypes has been contributed in the twentieth century by the work of Carl G. Jung.

In speaking of this great psychologist — one of the shapers of the thinking of this century — it must be remembered that he was an enthusiastic student of the matters which concern us here. He gave deep and perceptive attention to various aspects of Qabalah, even though the kindred subject of Gnosticism was the one which offered him the richer mine in which to trace out and bring to light the forgotten treasures of the human imagination.

The existence of certain, at least, of the archetypes within the psyche, as well as externally to it, is stated in one text attributed to Hermes Trismegistus. The profound study of the matter which was made by Jung does not contradict, therefore, but supplements the work of his predecessors in this tradition.

Jung writes with an acute awareness of his position, neither as theologian nor as philosopher, but as physician. His inquiry is not concerned with the Divine Mind or the archetypes as subsisting in it, but with what he perceives of the influences which impinge upon the human psyche.

One of the greatest of these influences — the greater because generally undiscerned in its activity — is the Collective Unconscious: that powerful substratum of living awareness which at its deepest levels links all existence, then all life and, arising from that, the particular Collective Unconscious of the human race. At that deep level no experience, no emotional attitude is lost, but according to intensity and duration will influence the whole Unconscious which, in a crisis, can arise to become a powerful motivation.

It is in this powerful substratum of human awareness that Jung perceives the archetypes to have their place: primarily as abstract and imageless forces (as are the archetypes in the Divine Mind) but inevitably endowed with form as they rise into the consciousness of a nation, of a religious group, of an individual. In that arising development we are no longer considering pure archetypes, but "archetypal images".

The "being-act" of the archetypes

It is noteworthy that the archetypes can exist as specific nuclei in the Divine Mind (and can likewise exist as such, by reflection from the Divine Mind, in the Collective Unconscious) because of their inner dynamism. Each archetype represents an act, or a condition of being, which of itself implies a relationship towards some other condition of being.

If we suppose the archetype of "table", for example, it is irrelevant which of the many kinds of table our imagination presents to us. Essentially, a table exists for the purpose of supporting something — primarily food — which is placed upon it. Whatever material it may be made from, in whatever form, a table must be suited to fulfil its purpose as a support.

This is implied in the incident in book VII of Vergil's *Aenid*, describing the fulfilment of a prophecy which had been made previously to Aeneas by the shade of his father Anchises, "You will eat your tables".

Lacking other expedients for eating, Aeneas and his fellow wanderers, resting under a tree, pile their food upon robust flat-breads. It is the boy Ascanius who cries playfully, "We are eating our tables!" — his youthful directness and purity of perception coming close for the moment to the elevated vision of the venerable shade.

Archetypes and gods

It is a comparable case with the great archetypes which have in different times and cultures been discerned by humankind. That of the Great Mother can be instanced. She has been imaged as a female sphynx with the tail of a dragon, as a many-breasted woman, as a woman crowned and enthroned — but the reality which different peoples have perceived, and which they have clothed in so many images, is one single great spiritual and imageless reality within the Divine Mind.

The development of a god is a process which becomes clearer if we trace its upward course.

A group of people, let us say, feel moved to worship by their contemplation of a certain sublime concept. Equally they may have been moved by practical needs to seek, emotionally and spiritually, for a divine provider or protector of a particular type: to bring them perhaps victory in war, or prosperity in peace. They image to themselves such a being, and according to the traditions of their race they create a mode of worship for this being.

The creative imagination of the devotees will shape in the astral world (the World of Yetzirah) a likeness, more or less distinctly formulated, of the deity as they conceive of it; and this likeness will become a focal point for the emotions and impulses generated in their worship. These emotions and impulses likewise are of the World of Yetzirah.

Even at this stage, a certain degree of power will become discernible in the cult, but this power is only derived from the energies projected by the emotions and impulses of the devotees themselves. It will therefore be transitory and inconsistent. The astral shape which will be imbued with these energies will lack permanence and, should the cult fail, will ultimately fall back into the general flow of the astral light; but in certain circumstances an astral shape animated in this way can outlast the cult itself for a very considerable time.

However, we can suppose that among the emotions and impulses of the devotees whose activities we have been following, there are some — perhaps many — which rise above the astral level by reason of their aspiration and close affinity to one or more of the divine archetypes: that of Justice for example, or that of Mercy, or of Love.

The Four Worlds and the Dynamic Archetypes

To describe these archetypes simply as "attributes" of deity is to be in danger of missing their essentially **dynamic** character. Being divine in origin, it is of their nature not merely to exist, but to act. They are a part of the divine nature itself, living and potent. Therefore when, over a period of time, human creativity, fervour and aspiration have prepared in Yetzirah a divine likeness which is a worthy vehicle and of adequate sephirothic purity, a reciprocal action takes place between that form and its archetype in Atziluth. From this reciprocal action there shines forth in Briah a glorious deity, a true god, sentient, sublimely infused with the power of its divine archetype.

In this process, in which the initial divine likeness has been reflected upwards, as it were, into the higher World and glorified, the primal astral vehicle is not destroyed but continues to exist in Yetzirah, where it is further empowered by its rapport with the higher Briatic level.

Properly to be considered as native to the World of Briah, the god is able to manifest at that level by its powers, or through its splendidly-divine Briatic godform. In this World the god communicates with those devotees who can be aware of it through their higher faculties; but it is able to manifest also in the World of Yetzirah (and even in certain circumstances in Assiah) through its astral image, its Yetziratic godform. This lower level of manifestation, though subsidiary to the divine presence centred in Briah, has generally been the more renowned and, by the wider increase of popular devotion, has done much to strengthen the interchange of archetypal and Yetziratic power.

This is the authentic teaching of the Qabalah concerning the nature of the gods. Some of the essential characteristics of the Worlds of Briah and Yetzirah, both in their own nature and in their relationship to human activity and development, may be perceived herein; but the brief account of those two Worlds which follows may serve to amplify matters.

Dwellers in the World of Briah

Among those who by nature inhabit the World of Briah are the wonderful beings whom we call the archangels. Truly, there is nothing in their nature which is not divine, but they are not of the World of Atziluth because they are living beings "sent forth" as the highest messengers of the divine will; it is therefore a part of their function to be capable of manifestation in power and in form, each archangel representing a separate aspect of the divine nature.

Briah is also named **the World of Mind**. As such, it is the level of the glorious and untrammelled action of the enlightened human mind, the action which is often described, and rightly, as "inspired". This does not imply a discounting of the normal processes of logical thought, but rather the brilliant effects produced through and beyond those processes by the enhanced perceptions on which they can now base their work.

In its best development, the attainment of this state is through a developed contact with the highest level of the psyche: nevertheless, a primary function of the gods is to "mediate" for their devotees so as to supplement their ordinary human faculties with some effects of this level of true inspiration: deep insight, prophetic knowledge, perception of truth.

The magical World of Yetzirah

An immense amount could be written concerning the World of Yetzirah, the astral world.

It extends to such height that among its inhabitants are numbered those whom we name the angels. It also includes those whom we name the elementals: from noble and powerful beings, through the simple nature spirits in their myriad forms, down to the deformed and hideous beings of the gross astral region.

The World of Yetzirah is the field of most vital activity for the practitioner of magic or psychism, it is also a region of seductive and perilous fascination. It holds scenes of exquisite beauty, and pits of repellent horror. One of its titles is **the Formative World**, for it holds the images of phenomena and happenings which will at a future time be realized in the material world. It is called **the World of Illusion**, on account of the extremely pliant and constantly flowing nature of its substance, the Astral Light. Many of its numberless images are fantastic and fleeting, while others, seemingly more stable, will yet find no realisation whatever in the material world.

Among these last are the idle dreams and the feeble wishes of numberless beings, human and other, as well as those tentative formulations of natural causality which, in the event, will be overridden by some more potent cause.

However, Yetzirah is also the World of truly creative imagination, one of our most precious faculties. With this, and with the ever changing beauty of the Astral Light which can give joy and refreshment to all who learn to know it in waking reverie or sleeping dream, the World of Yetzirah is an indispensable part of living experience.

CHAPTER 3
THE CONTRIBUTION OF THE HERMETIC CORPUS

A late Egyptian source

The important body of writings ascribed to Hermes Trismegistus must in its early days have been extensive. It originates as a collection mainly in the Greek language, partly in Latin, from about the third century of the Christian era in Egypt. There is nothing, however, either Christian or Jewish to be traced, either in the origin or in the religious attitudes of these writings.

None the less, during some six hundred years previously — since about 350 B.C. — portions of the Hebrew Bible had been progressively translated into Greek in Alexandria, to be amalgamated at last into the complete Septuagint. It seems unlikely therefore that the pagans of the Greek culture of northern Africa were entirely unaware of the narratives contained in the Jewish scriptures, although the intrinsic religious traditions remained alien to them. The Hermetic writings bear witness to a mentality with quite other, more speculative, preoccupations.

These are the works of a number of anonymous authors, resident in Egypt and probably in the main Egyptian by race. They were evidently immersed in the Greek philosophies which were then current — Stoic, Aristotelian, but above all Platonist — which they spontaneously, often unconsciously, grafted upon the rootstock of their native thinking, the ancient magico-religious wisdom of Egypt.

The now legendary teacher who is known to us only by the honorific title of Hermes Thrice-greatest, may or may not have left authentic written works. In any case it would be impossible to trace them among the copious writings — themselves now fragmented — of his disciples and admirers. What remains however, the *Corpus*

Hermeticum as we have it, is the unique record of a vital current in the development of Western mystical philosophy.

We can say with certainty that these anonymous Egyptian writers had no intention of claiming any dogmatic authority for divine revelation in their texts. No such concept formed a part of their mental background. It was otherwise, however, with the Jewish, Christian and Moslem readers of later centuries into whose hands fell these scripts of elder wisdom.

A basis of mystical philosophy

Here these readers found a basis of mystical philosophy which was lacking in their own scriptures, but which yet was in great measure strangely congenial to them. The hermetic texts found a new authority, a status of high veneration, not indeed as revealed doctrine but as indispensable supplementary teachings. Eagerly they were searched by scholars of every persuasion, to restore to the new gathering of wisdom which was being made — including the developing Qabalah — those treasures of human perception and understanding which had been lost from the heritage of the western world.

The beginnings in the *Poimandres*

The first text of the Corpus Hermeticum, the *Poimandres*, is of particular interest and also has doubtless been the most influential historically of the Hermetic texts. It opens with a not unusual declaration, that the author is recording the contents of a vision. In this vision, he relates, a being of immeasurable magnitude appeared to him and, upon being questioned, declared, "I am Poimandres" - that is, the Shepherd - "the Mind of the Supreme."

The seer expresses his desire to know those things which are true, and to comprehend their nature, and to gain knowledge of God.

His desire is granted. At the first his vision is filled with a genial Light, bringing him gladness and wonder. Then follows a presentation of the origin of all things, for there is darkness and a substance resembling turbulent water which moans and cries. The Light also makes utterance, giving forth a sacred Word which rests upon the waters. The four elements — fire, air, water and earth —

are brought forth from this chaotic and turbulent "first matter" immediately at the resting thereon of the Word.

Poimandres explains that the Light is himself, the Divine Mind, and that the utterance made by the Light is therefore the offspring of the Divine Mind and is the Son of God. The Mind and its utterance together constitute Life.

Having met the seer's eyes in an awe-inspiring gaze, Poimandres now bids him fix his attention upon the Light. He looks, and sees mentally that the Light is composed of numberless Potencies, it having become a world of order although without material confines. Poimandres tells him, "You have known in your mind the archetypal plan *(to archetypon eidos)* antecedent to the beginnings and boundless." *(Poimandres 1—8)*

The seer asks Poimandres as to the origin of the first principles of nature and is told that they stem from the colloquy of God with the Word, being the actualisation of the beautiful kosmos of the divine thought.

The Divine Mind, the "First Mind", is now described as producing, by the Word, a "Second Mind", the *Demiourgos*, the Maker, who in turn produces seven great governors. Together the Demiourgos and the Word imbue the seven governors with vitality and movement.

* * *

This passage, with the inner perceptions which it delineates, takes a paramount place in the development of subsequent mystical traditions. Its main points should be noted:

1   The Light is identical with the Divine Mind, which is none other than the Supreme God.

This is confirmed in a slightly later passage referring to "the primal Mind, which is Life and Light" *(Poimandres 9.)*

2   The Divine Mind gives forth an utterance which is described as its "Son", but this without breaking the unity of the Divine Being.

This is illustrated in *Poimandres* 6 by the case that a man's thoughts or words do not disrupt the unity of his being. (Augustine appears to have had this passage in mind when formulating his own acute perception of the "first trine" in the faculties of the soul, in his *De Trinitate*.)

3   The Light is then seen to be filled with numberless potencies: the world of the archetypes, entirely spiritual, but with ordered plan.

All this activity is within what, in qabalistic terminology, we name the World of Atziluth. A total and most significant distinction can be noted here, between the teeming but ordered archetypes of the divine plan and the barren crying and moaning turbulence of the primal chaos. The utterance, the Son, of the Light is defined as a "Word" in contrast to that inarticulate noise in which — to refer to a well-known alchemical concept — inchoate qualities which are afterwards brought to resolution battle against one other.

4   The First Mind produces by its Word the Second Mind, the Demiourgos, which in turn brings forth seven governors.

This Second Mind, the Demiourgos, would in qabalistic thinking correspond to the Elohim, the "builder of the Worlds," who, having her essential being within the unity of Atziluth, establishes her creative work primarily in the life and organisation of the World of Briah. The seven governors are the seven anciently-known planetary powers, whose archetypes are here clothed in form by the activity of the demiurge.

5   By the action of the Second Mind and the Word, the governors are vitalised.

The seven, their archetypal powers thus called forth and implemented, are in their turn fertile and prolific, generating further forms at each level of being according to their own likenesses as the planetary powers.

The Great Inspiration

From this point the *Poimandres* moves on to the creation of the intelligences and living beings of the lower spheres, and to the creation of 'Man'. Then, in a simple theme of personal return to the celestial origins, it emphasises the need for true knowledge of the Self as a being of Life and Light whose source is the Divine Mind and whose goal is return thereto.

And, assuredly, it is in its statement that the higher intelligence belongs to the divinely intended completeness of human nature, and in its appeal for a true *gnosis* of the Self, that the *Poimandres* has most intensely gripped the mystical imagination of the western world. "From Life, the Soul", says the Shepherd, "and from Light, the Mind."

CHAPTER 4
TRADITIONS CONTINUED IN THE ZOHAR

On the manifestation of the Unmanifest

The *Poimandres,* and perhaps in particular the passage which we have considered in Chapter 3, has certainly been a potent seminal text influencing, directly and indirectly, much of the mystical thought of the western world. Its recognisable influence in the Zohar alone is considerable, and, without pursuing the effects of this into wider areas of thought, we are concerned to indicate some particular relationships between the Zohar itself and the text we have examined from the *Poimandres,* as being of considerable importance to the student of the Qabalah whether from the mystical or the magical viewpoint.

This is not a matter of the perception of any simple literary connection between the two texts. The author of the Greco-Egyptian text may perhaps, indeed, have met with some part of the Hebrew scriptures, but his writing remains true to its native mode of speculative philosophy; the author of the Aramaic text, steeped in the Hebrew scriptures with their doctrines and traditions, has taken the imprint of the *Poimandres* to an extent of which he may or may not have been consciously aware. That is the nearest we can come to establishing a direct link between the two pieces of work. The value of the comparison lies in the additional light which each work throws into the depth of meaning of the other.

I

Our perception of Godhead

The passage in the Zohar for comparison at this point is contained in the commentary upon the Book of Exodus. It naturally takes up the question as to how the Invisible was perceived by Moses, and then proceeds to consider — as does the *Poimandres* — the design and system of the manifestation of God in his attributes, without outrage either to his transcendence or to his essential unity of being. In Zohar and *Poimandres* alike this is achieved through the instrumentality of a vehicle, a Word or Supernal Man, which, although capable of descent into manifestation, remains one in nature with the divine Unmanifest.

It is true that in Hebrew mystical thought, as shown explicitly in other passages of the Zohar, the Shekinah is one means of manifestation of the Holy One. But the Shekinah is manifest only to the delicate perceptions of the few: not in that manner is a means of enlightenment to be made accessible to humankind as a whole. Here, therefore, we have another instrument of manifestation: that which is designated as the Supernal Man.

This is for the Qabalist a topic of no merely theoretical interest. We return to it in a later chapter when we come to consider the dignity and powers of the human person. However, our purpose here is to examine the question proposed in the Zohar, as to how Divinity, by definition invisible and unknowable, had ever been discerned or known by humankind.

The Divine Chariot of Manifestation

This question is answered in part by the well-known argument that God is known by our recognition of his attributes and powers as these can be inferred from the phenomena of the universe around us. He is to be known also, the Zohar states, by the expression of certain of his attributes, and the conveyance of their powers, in the various Divine Names.

Above all this is the case with the Name which is rendered as YHVH, and with the individual letters (Yod, Heh, Vau, Heh) of which it is composed. The Zohar tells us that when God had formulated Supernal Man, the archetype not only of humankind but also of that store of divine concepts of which humankind is the reflection and counterpart, Supernal Man became the means of manifestation, *the chariot, in which the Holy One came down* through the Four Worlds to be known by humankind as YHVH.

This takes for granted two basic concepts of the psychology of the Zohar: first, the existence in each individual person of the nature of each of the Four Worlds; and secondly the fact that it is only through the existence of these four levels in ourselves that we are able to recognise the essence of each level in its cosmic and spiritual counterparts.

Supernal Man as the Divine Chariot

The outstanding point of contact between the line of thought in the *Poimandres* and that in the Zohar consists in the nature of the instrument by which the simple unity of the Divine Light is disclosed to humankind as a complex and active whole.

In the *Poimandres* the Divine Light gives forth an utterance, which is called the Son of the Light, and by this utterance the Four Elements are brought forth from primal chaos.

In the account from the Zohar the Supernal Man is brought into being. (Regarding the sonship of the Supernal Man, which is stated in an earlier portion of the Zohar, see our Chapter 10.) The revelation of God, in his name YHVH, is then accomplished through the vehicle of Supernal Man, "the Chariot of the Holy One."

The Tetragrammaton in the Four Worlds

The descent of the Holy One, in his powers and attributes, through the Four Worlds is traditionally expressed by the allocation of the letters of the Tetragrammaton, YHVH, as follows:

The letter Y, the Hebrew letter Yod, remains with Atziluth, for it here symbolises the active creative power of the Supernal Father.

The first H, the Hebrew letter Heh which represents a window, is attributed to Briah, the World of Mind, for it is a "window between the Worlds" and through Mind we have our apperception of the Divine.

The letter V, the Hebrew letter Vau, represents a nail; here it is attributed to Yetzirah, for in that "World behind the tangible World" divine force is as it were pinned in the service of Matter.

The second H is again a window of hope and aspiration for the dwellers on Earth looking outwards and upwards, because in wonder and awe at the manifest universe we find our beginning of wisdom. It is attributed to the World of Assiah.

It must be borne in mind that although in the *Poimandres* the "Son" is not anthropomorphised, in the Zohar the "chariot of descent" is the concept of human nature entire and perfect.

The sacred name YHVH is taken, in the Zohar generally, to correspond to whatever symbolism may bring the Incomprehensible closer to the comprehension of the human mind. Thus the Tetragrammaton is related variously to the Sephiroth, to the framework of the spiritual and material universe, to the Four Elements and to much else. **So far as humankind is concerned, human nature itself and its perceptions are inevitably the vehicle by which the self-revelation of the Holy One may be cognized.** This condition is implicit, so clearly as to need no precise statement, in the thought of the Zohar.

In the present instance the letters YHVH are related, as we have said, to the Four Worlds of existence. For human nature has essentially its own correspondence to the Four Worlds: in them each individual person has being. The material body manifestly belongs to the World of Assiah; it is built and nourished with the components of the material universe. The emotional-instinctual nature infuses the astral body: this level of the psyche is of one substance with the Astral World, the World of Yetzirah. The mind in its full development belongs to, and inhabits, the World of Briah; while the spirit, the divine and highest level of the inner life, belongs to and subsists always in the World of Atziluth.

The Microcosm and the Four Elements

It is for this reason — the extension of the individual life through the Four Worlds — that the individual person is termed the "microcosm", that is, a universe in miniature. Besides this, the Zohar does not fail to indicate the relationship of the levels of the psyche to the Elements.

The Zoharic commentary on Genesis presents the levels of the psyche as an upward, progressively inward, stair. Lowest and outermost is the *Nephesh* (the emotional-instinctual nature), which abides in the astral life-current and whose attribution is **Water**. The Nephesh is given purpose by the *Ruach* (rational and intellectual mind), the midmost faculty whose attribution is **Air**. Above the Ruach is the *Neshamah* (the spirit or higher self), the pinnacle and the inmost centre of the psyche whose attribution is **Fire**. The Neshamah draws the Ruach upwards to itself as, one might put it, a fire attracts and draws upwards a current of air, and embracing the Ruach gives spiritual life to both it and the Nephesh.

The physical body, the earthly habitation of these components of the psyche, is the *Guph,* whose attribution is **Earth**.

Considerations

To summarise therefore the attributions of the Divine Name, including both those proper to Supernal Man and those relating to microcosmic humankind, we have:

Letter of Divine Name	World	Level of personality	Element
Y	Atziluth	Neshamah	Fire
H	Briah	Ruach	Air
V	Yetzirah	Nephesh	Water
H	Assiah	Guph	Earth

This relationship of the Tetragrammaton with the Worlds, the levels of the psyche, and the Four Elements, throws light upon the meaning of the Zohar concerning the revelation of the Most High by the vehicle of Supernal Man, through the name YHVH. It also illustrates the parallel between this text and those words of the *Poimandres* given in Chapter 3, which indicate that the Four Elements are brought forth from the chaotic *prima materia* immediately after the resting thereon of the sacred Word (the Son).

However, the Zoharic perception of the approach, through Supernal Man our archetype, of humankind at large to the divine nature as manifest in the four Worlds in which we exist — and to the four elements which compose our material being and by which our psychic and spiritual being is symbolised — this, with the inference that in the mode of divine descent there lies also for us a way of ascent, must arrest our attention beyond the subject of the remote origin of things.

There stands out therefore among the considerations which appear in the above, the vision of human progress and destiny which, through the Hermetica and the Zohar, permeates Qabalistic thought: a vision transcultural in its origins, wide in its influence, and sublime in its implications.

II

The Ten, the Three and the Seven

In both *Poimandres* and Zohar we are introduced to a total of ten divinely-originating units which are grouped, not symmetrically but as three and seven. There are points of particular significance in comparing the interpretations of these numerical concepts made by *Poimandres* and Zohar respectively, but before proceeding to review these interpretations we may notice the appearance of the ten, the three and the seven in other writings.

The Primal Ten

It would be impossible to set a time of origin for the establishment of ten as a special number. Just as children still learn to reckon by counting their fingers, so at whatever remote period the human race first discovered its ability to count, doubtless the digits of the two hands became the first instruments of that art.

One might therefore expect that the number five would be established as a special number before the ten. But in the early numerical systems of Babylon, Phoenicia and (excepting the hieratic script) Egypt, ten was the lowest number above unity to be given a distinctive sign, five being represented simply as three plus two.

Pythagorean influence

The tenets of the mysterious religious-philosophical society which was founded by Pythagoras in the latter part of the sixth century B.C., exercised so far as they became known a great influence in the western world of their time. Their authority however probably came largely from the fact that they gave form and logic to notions which were already current in the developing thought of every culture.

This is conspicuous in their development of thought upon the number ten. They held the ten to be sacred, and attached a particular power and sanctity to its arrangement as the *tetraktys*

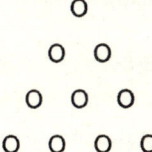

Much reflection upon this figure is possible. It can for instance be interpreted to signify that from the one proceed the two, from the two the three, and from the three the four; and — since ten is the perfect number which comprises, or at least symbolises, the totality of all things — the emanation of the All from the One. **Again, if the figure is divided horizontally, the upper portion comprises three units and the lower portion seven.**

From these, and other seemingly simple observations on the *tetraktys*, profound conclusions have been drawn.

The One and the Ten

The Greek philosopher Aristotle (of whom more in Chapter 9), born in the year 384-3 B.C., discerned all existent being to be susceptible of consideration under ten heads — the famous "ten categories" — substance, quantity, quality, relationship, place, time, situation, possession, activity, passivity. It is observable that of these categories, the first three are internal to whatever may be the subject under consideration, the other seven concern its involvement with the world around it. In the tenth century A.D., if the categories had not been specifically introduced earlier into Jewish thought, they were introduced at that time by the writer Saadiah.

In the third century A.D., a Jewish teacher of Babylon known simply as Rav writes as of an accepted fact, "Ten are the qualities through which the world is created." His list of those qualities is given by Gershom G. Scholem in *Major trends in Jewish Mysticism*; it is not the list of the ten as the Sephiroth have since been named and standardised, but the statement of the creative qualities as being ten is relevant for us.

In seeking an early episode to illustrate the authority and dignity of the number ten, the example of the Ten Commandments seems an obvious choice.

This subject is one of great Qabalistic interest but is by no means as simple as may at first appear. Neither in Hebrew nor in Greek scriptural texts are the ten Utterances referred to as commandments: they are, simply and literally, the "Ten Words" (Hebrew, *OShRTh HDBRIM;* Greek, *ta deka hemata*). Furthermore, in the whole bible only three times are they described as being ten in number: Exodus 34:28, Deuteronomy 4:13 and 10:4.

Nowhere, not even in the passages above cited, are the Utterances numbered from one to ten. Although it is agreed that they are ten, the manner in which they are so, and their probable allocation to the two stone tablets, has called forth varying opinions among writers of different religions and traditions, different times and places.

The Dividing of the Ten

A number of early Aramaic scripts exist, which paraphrase or interpret some part of the Hebrew scriptures. These are the *Targums.*

Probably the earliest known Targum is that of Jonathan ben Uzziel of Babylon, written between the third and fourth centuries A.D. In contrast to the prevalent arrangement of the Hebrew text of the Commandments, ben Uzziel amalgamates the injunction to the sole worship of the God of Israel with the prohibition of graven images. He thus makes reverence to the divine name the subject of the second Word, and observance of the Sabbath the subject of the third.

Within about fifty years of ben Uzziel's work, St. Augustine of Hippo reports the existence of this interpretation, and makes a consequent suggestion that the first three Words as thereby enumerated were inscribed upon the first of the tablets of Sinai, with the remaining seven Words upon the second tablet.

The Three and the Seven in *Poimandres* and Zohar

In the establishment of the comprehensive series of ten, and its organization into the groups of three and seven, we may certainly conjecture Pythagorean and Aristotelian influences in the cultures of Egypt, Babylon and Alexandria in the early centuries of the common era. Whatever the origin of these concepts, their impulse was strong enough to influence the basic plan of ideas in the *Poimandres* and thence, in due course, to reinforce and systematise for the Zoharic thinkers a plan of development which would already be in some part familiar to them from other sources. Certainly this plan of development occupies a notable place in the growing patterns of Qabalistic thought we are now tracing.

In the *Poimandres,* beyond making it clear that none of the developments in any way impair the divine unity, the author shows no great interest in his demonstration that the primal movements within the Divine Light result in its becoming threefold within that unity: the trine consisting of the Light itself, the Word and the Demiourgos. Certainly the emanation of the Word which is the "Son" is emphasised as a matter of paramount importance, and necessarily so: it is through this event that the subsequent phenomena are produced, which constitute all the knowable links between the One — the Divine Light — and the Many among which we are included. Of this chain of phenomena, the production of the seven governors is a vital feature.

Following its presentation of Supernal Man as the Chariot of the Holy One, the Zoharic commentary on Exodus presents the Ten Sephiroth of the Tree of Life — the great Qabalistic symbol of the divine attributes with the qualities and powers in which they are manifest through the Worlds — in the image of a series of water courses springing from a single Source. In this system the three supernal Sephiroth are represented as the **Fountainhead**, its **Outpouring**, and the **Sea** which is formed thereby: then seven **Watercourses** which flow from the Sea represent the seven lower Sephiroth.

Thus in *Poimandres* and Zohar alike do we have our tenfold system presenting the primal and divine trine of powers from which is originated the subsidiary series of seven; and while the development from the basic pattern differs necessarily from the one system to the other, the evident relationship between the two systems is none the less noteworthy.

The *Poimandres,* and it can be said the *Hermetic Corpus* as it survives to us, makes a wide survey of the creative work of the Kosmos, not as something completed in a remote past but as an ongoing process, in which the return of Man to Life and Light is intimately involved. In the Zohar, as in Qabalistic thought and practice generally, the concept of the Ten Sephiroth as an ever creative dynamism in the universe of which our own nature is an integral part, stands as a central, vital and inspiring reality.

CHAPTER 5
THE TEN SEPHIROTH

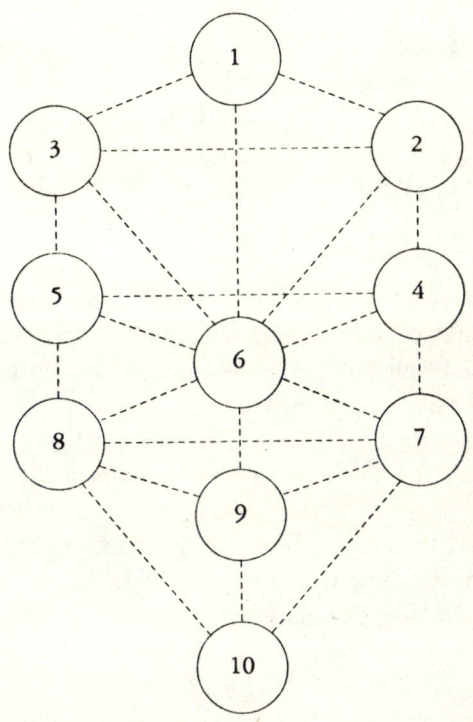

The Ten Sephiroth

The Ten Sephiroth form the basic pattern of the **Tree of Life**, as illustrated above. Each Sephirah is a dynamic mode of being, the character of which is reflected in, and is influenced by, its place in the scheme of the Ten. Each Sephirah has its unique name, and each is made known to us in particular qualities, or in symbols of those qualities, throughout the Four Worlds. The following table shows the names of the Sephiroth in Hebrew and in English, with an indication of the character of each.

1.	KETHER	The Crown	Total unity
2.	CHOKMAH	Wisdom	Expansion
3.	BINAH	Understanding	Condensation
4.	CHESED	Mercy, Magnificence	Order
5.	GEBURAH	Strength	Energy
6.	TIPHARETH	Beauty	Equilibrium
7.	NETZACH	Victory	Combination
8.	HOD	Splendour	Analysis
9.	YESOD	Foundation	Conception
10.	MALKUTH	Kingdom	Realisation

Behind the Beginning

We are proceeding to an account of the emanation of the Sephiroth — the beginning of our universe at its highest spiritual level, from Kether. The Qabalah however does not regard the spiritual beginning of our universe as the commencement of all activity within the divine unity, although it is almost the highest and most subtle level which mystical perception has been able to communicate.

Those remote levels above Kether represent a state which passes almost beyond the scope of human language. It has no place in magical work or training; but, to complete the record, here is a brief account of Negative Existence.

There is no reason to consider the levels of that existence as "negative" in themselves. Rather we must suppose them as phases of the most dynamic spiritual potency. But our mental processes are formed within, and by, our universe, and we can frame no clear perceptions of the higher level beyond it. Mathematically we may say that the higher level approaches, and touches, a point "zero" from which its energies break through into a newer dimension, which is ours and which to us is "positive".

Three degrees of negative existence are sometimes described. All that is relevant for the student's attention however is the single fact of that existence, and the related name **Ain Soph**, meaning "Without Limit". This does not mean only that the divine being is infinite: that is always true, but as regards the phase of negative existence it means also that there is no manifestation, there are neither attributions nor definitions, and therefore there are no implied limitations. For, in the structure of language, to "define" must inevitably be to impute a limit.

At a certain point, we are told, a tension of divine being breaks through from that state into the dimension of reality as we know it: a reality as yet entirely spiritual, and now pervaded by divine being as we may comprehend it — the Supreme God, the Divine Mind, the World of Atziluth, they are truly one — and within this unity there originate as archetypes, to be sent forth by emanation, the other Worlds and the Sephiroth.

The Emanation of the Sephiroth

Intrinsically, from their very origin within the Divine Mind, the Sephiroth are considered as developing — emanating — one from another in a definite self-balancing order.

The diagram following, "the Lightning Flash", specifically illustrates the sequence of the emanations.

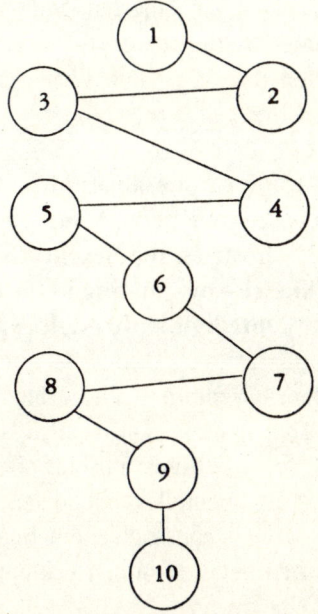

Sometimes in older depictions of this formulation, the Lightning Flash is shown at its beginning, at Kether, to issue from the mouth of a venerable head with flowing hair and beard. The meaning is clear: the whole Tree of Life, and each Sephirah in its turn, is "uttered" by the First Cause, the Most Holy Ancient One.

Kether is the first Sephirah. It is "pure light", a glory of which the essential quality is Unity: a unity perfect and unassailable, but within itself life-giving, fecund. Kether in Atziluth is the source of the Worlds of positive existence and contains all the other Sephiroth in potential.

Chokmah, the second Sephirah, is the incipient "being" of the universe, the Sphere of the *logoi spermatikoi*, of the Ideas which are the seeds of all life whether spiritual, astral or material: it is the Fatherhood in the divine nature. Fulfilling that quality, Chokmah, supernal Wisdom, transmits to Binah the stupendous energies received from Kether.

Binah, the third Sephirah, manifests the quality of Motherhood in the divine nature. Binah is supernal Understanding, the receptive wisdom. Impregnated by the power of Chokmah, she comprehends and gives formation to every thing which shall have birth in the worlds of light and life.

These three — Kether, Chokmah and Binah — are the supernal Sephiroth. Binah is the wellspring of form at every level of being: from this point downwards, the Sephiroth show forth qualities which, although likewise originating in the divine attributes, are for us more plainly intelligible through experience.

Chesed, the fourth Sephirah, can be interpreted as Mercy or as Loving Kindness. The Sephirah is also called **Gedulah**, Magnificence. The Sephirah shows forth the divine attribute of magnanimity, of a liberal and loving bestowal from boundless abundance. Its expansiveness is in contrast to the form-giving, constrictive function of Binah; but it is also a reflection and reinterpretation in more comprehensible terms of the paternal quality of Chokmah.

Geburah, the fifth Sephirah, is Strength, which is energy channeled and ordered; it gives tautness and direction to the impulses of the universe, whether spiritual, mental, or tending into manifestation. As transformer of that which may be chaotic or may miss its purpose, Geburah also represents divine justice. It reflects and gives a new purpose to the containing and formative powers of Binah, and provides a necessary factor of balance to the liberality of the fourth Sephirah.

Tiphareth, Beauty, the sixth Sephirah, unites in its own harmony those aspects of the divine nature which the higher Sephiroth had diversified in their particular modes of being. In a special way, Tiphareth is the focal centre of the Tree of Life, and is for the Sephiroth below it not only a restatement of the unity of Kether, but a more discernible presentment of its glory, a gentler transmission of its vital force.

Netzach, the seventh Sephirah, receives and transmits the current of mighty energy conditioned by the glory of Tiphareth. In Netzach, Victory, the divine life is made manifest in the abounding love and intense vitality of natural existence: for that which we call "Nature", which is the very being of Netzach, has its place in each one of the Worlds.

Hod is the balance to Netzach: the forces combining in this eighth Sephirah do not make for harmony. While all things are known as one by the Divine Mind, likewise each thing is known separately. Hod divides and analyses; it also concentrates and crystallises, yet even in these processes it shows forth the diverse virtues of that which is produced. The Splendour which gives its title is that of a dazzling iridescence, an intellectual quality playing lightly over all that it touches.

Yesod, the ninth Sephirah, is the Foundation. Blending the influences of Tiphareth, Netzach and Hod, it gives expression to the infinitely varied creativity of the divine nature, no aspect of which eclipses another although, in the lower Worlds, their multiform facets can only be shown forth as changefulness. But always the function of Yesod is to concentrate the power of the received sephirothic influences, adding to them its own brightness and vital conceptual power, then projecting them in this intensity into Malkuth.

Malkuth, the Kingdom, is the tenth Sephirah, called in the Zohar "the Female". Malkuth is "the receptacle of the influences of all the Lights", completing the primal pattern of the Ten Sephiroth. It appears as a pendant to Yesod, or to the entire Tree of Life, representing the interaction and resolution of the sephirothic forces at whatever level of existence the Tree is considered.

Ever-repeating pattern

As the sephirothic influences descend through the Worlds of Briah and Yetzirah to their manifestation in the material universe of Assiah, they are progressively less recognisable as aspects of deity and are more readily defined simply as modes of being — of thought, of feeling, of action or effect.

Each of these modes of being in descending through the Worlds keeps, nevertheless, its essential identity, an identity which is often more easily perceived than defined.

Taking as an example the quality of beauty: besides the primal divine attribute of beauty there can be discerned intellectual beauty, the beauty of great works of art and of music, the beauty of the natural cosmos, voluptuous beauty and other kinds however we may classify them. Yet in all we recognise the "voice" bespeaking beauty. Therein is the essential sephirothic quality.

Seen thus, the pattern of the Tree of Life is a continually repeating pattern, as a whole or in parts. The entire pattern, with its descent through the Worlds, exists in ourselves: a fact of paramount importance in both mystical and magical development.

It is also recognised that there is "a Tree within each Sephirah": that is, that within each mode of being there are comprised, besides its own intrinsic nature, aspects of all the other modes of being. This is very perceptible in human experience. A student's commitment to his chosen subject of study (Hod) can develop the fervour of a religious devotion (Chesed), while the perceptions of a lover (Netzach) can be as exact and as piercing as a surgeon's scalpel (Geburah).

CHAPTER 6
BINAH AND THE SEVEN PLANETARY POWERS

Taking count of the Seven

As we have seen, Binah is imaged by the Zohar as a Sea from which issue seven Watercourses, these representing the seven lower Sephiroth of the Tree of Life: Chesed, Geburah, Tiphareth, Netzach, Hod, Yesod and Malkuth.

While in the *Poimandres* the "Seven Governors" relate to the seven planets of the Ptolemaic system, the seven lower Sephiroth do not directly correspond to that series. The seven planets themselves indeed have of their own right their place in Qabalistic thought and practice, and the powers and influences of the planets can be recognised in the characters of the related Sephiroth; but the presence on the Tree of the Sephirah Malkuth, of which the corresponding planet is Earth, gives at once a different reckoning of the Seven. The total number of the Sephiroth is maintained as ten by the dual allocation of the third Sephirah: in its higher aspect it is the sphere of the Elohim, the Supernal Mother, in its lower aspect that of the planet Saturn, which has ever been recognised as the most sublime of all the planetary spheres. This dual allocation is no mere compromise: it is the showing forth and expression of a great mystical power, seen both in its cosmic and downwards-regarding, and in its micrococosmic and upwards-aspiring, aspects.

Trismegistus on the Planetary Powers

In a precious fragment ascribed to Trismegistus himself in the Hermetic corpus, the seven luminaries are given by their Greek names, with brief descriptions of their respective roles as the governors of our destinies on earth (Stobaeus I.5,14):

"Seven wandering stars turn in a circle at the sill of Olympus, and among them turns endlessly Time for ever returning.* These are the seven: Mene (the Moon) light of the night, sedate Kronos (Saturn), joyous Helios (the Sun), Paphie (Venus) to whom the nuptial bed pays homage,** bold Ares (Mars), Hermes (Mercury) of powerful wings, and Zeus (Jupiter) supreme Father of all births, from whom Nature receives life."

The planets are here named in no regular order since this is a metrical composition, but the passage in which these lines occur has importance for us: the poet proceeds to state that these same cosmic powers exist also within us, and that we inhale the special influence of each of them with that "aether" which is the breath of life of the universe. He then declares what inner gift we receive from each planetary power. The list is not a remarkable one: but tears are the gift of Kronos.

That the planetary powers exist as a reality which not only encompasses us but is a vital part of our inner being, is a theme which has been taken up by other thinkers; it is a recognised and necessary foundation of the magical art. Between this teaching of Trismegistus and that of the Zohar, that the archetypal powers in their Atziluthic purity condition our primal essence before ever we come into incarnate life, there is entire harmony.

The Planets and the Sephiroth

Regarding the sequence of the luminaries as presented in the Ptolemaic system of astronomy, it is noteworthy that this is preserved in the Qabalistic sequence of the Sephiroth. Thus Saturn, which occupies the seventh sphere in the Ptolemaic system, corresponds in the Qabalah to the third Sephirah, Binah, below which are reckoned the lower Sephiroth; Jupiter, of the sixth sphere, corresponds to the fourth Sephirah, Chesed; Mars, of the fifth sphere, to the fifth Sephirah, Geburah; the Sun holds the fourth sphere and

---

* Here, certainly, is the source of the motto to which Lorenzo the Magnificent, great pupil of Marsilio Ficino, gave such poignant significance: *Le tems revient*, "The Time Returns".

** The Greek text of this phrase is hopelessly confused. The interpretation given above seems the most likely.

corresponds to the sixth Sephirah, Tiphareth; Venus holds the third sphere and corresponds to the seventh Sephirah, Netzach; Mercury holds the second sphere and corresponds to the eighth Sephirah, Hod; and the Moon, being the nearest to Earth, holds the first sphere and corresponds to the ninth Sephirah, Yesod.

The planet Earth corresponds to the tenth Sephirah, Malkuth. It thus has no place in the ancient sequence of the spheres; but Malkuth is the last and the completing Sephirah of the "seven lower Sephiroth" of the Zohar.

The enigma of Binah

At a deep level, the two aspects of Binah, the supernal and the planetary, are united. The Zohar refers in various contexts to Binah as a sea, and one of her symbols is indeed the dark and bitter ocean from which however all earthly life has arisen. "Tears are the gift of Kronos", and as is often the case, the condition of the devotee is reflected in the imagery attributed to the corresponding aspect of Deity. The male Saturnian image is often one of sombre age. For the female image, the great engraver Albrecht Dürer sought to convey something of its significance in his *Melancholia I*, the dejected figure with direful countenance, the compasses of the architect at her feet. Traditions both religious and esoteric have for the most part dealt more gently with the darker image of the Supernal Mother, but that harsh depiction is not without significance to us. As is recounted in our Chapter 10, the Zohar also tells of the Elohim, the Mother, as the architect fulfilling the mind of supernal Wisdom, the Father. This echoes closely one of the sources of the tradition we are tracing: a scriptural source which involves a curious feature of biblical Hebrew.

The Sorrowful Mother

In four places in the Book of Proverbs — chapters 1:20, 5:1, 9:1 and 24:7, the word denoting personified Wisdom is not *chakmah*, the feminine singular noun which normally signifies wisdom in the abstract: it is *chakmoth*, a feminine plural noun formed from *chakim*, the masculine singular noun for a sage or teacher of wisdom.

Although plural in form, *chakmoth* is in this context employed altogether as a singular noun; thus we have "her house", etc., in the

Hebrew just as we have in the English versions; as for example in the graphically evocative words of Proverbs 9:1, **Wisdom has built her house, she has hewn out her seven pillars.***

Without any doubt the word *chakmoth* is rightly translated here as "Wisdom". Why then has the author avoided, by an almost bizarre expedient, the use of the word *chakmah*? It seems certain that he has done so in the first place because that word is the name of the **second** Sephirah, Chokmah: the name, despite its feminine gender, of the great paternal Wisdom of the universe. The author of Proverbs has wished to make it quite explicit here that he writes of the maternal and formative Wisdom, the Creatrix, Binah: he has therefore chosen a word which is without any masculine connotation.

However, no matter what may have been the primary intention of the author, that is not the end of the story. In ancient Jewish history there were in reality, *chakmoth*. These were not teachers of wisdom, but women skilled in the art of lamentation, knowing the traditions, able to compose and sing funeral chants. They never worked singly, always in group. In Jeremiah 9:16 we find the *chakmoth* mentioned in that exact sense, where they are named in company with the *qunoth*, the "keeners", women whose function it was to wail and weep for the dead. In choosing the word *chakmoth*, may the author of Proverbs have been influenced by traditions of which he would surely have known, of the mourning of Astarte, of Ishtar and of Isis?

Be that as it may, because of those traditions, because of the Jewish custom and because of the use of the word in Proverbs, the idea of lamentation, of sorrowing, has attached itself almost inseparably to the figure of the feminine Wisdom; an idea supplemented by the subjective experience of certain mystics through the centuries.

A practical resolution

Without discounting a great mystery however, we can for most of the purposes of this book resolve the simpler matter of terminology. The Sephirah Binah comprises one aspect which the levels of

---

* These "seven pillars" are the seven lower Sephiroth.

ordinary human consciousness can comprehend, and another aspect which is wholly transcendental. To make a distinction therefore, we shall refer to the lower aspect of Binah as the Sphere of Planetary Saturn, but when we allude to Supernal Binah, the Sphere of the Supernal Mother, this will be stated explicitly.

This, it must be added, is a distinction which exists only in relation to human experience. But the integrity of the Sephirah Binah in itself is not sundered thereby.

CHAPTER 7
THE THREE COLUMNS

To interpret adequately the qualities and powers of the Sephiroth, each Sephirah must be considered not only in itself but in the pattern of relationships which are established by its position upon the Tree of Life. In this regard, the following formulation has an important place in the traditions of the Qabalah.

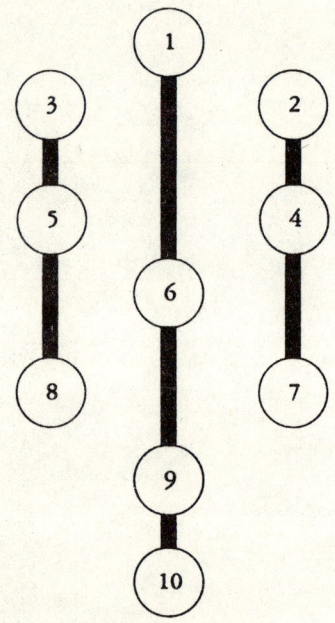

Significance of the Three Columns

The column on the left in this diagram is composed of the Sephiroth Binah, Geburah and Hod; that on the right is composed of Chokmah, Chesed and Netzach; while the central column is formed of Kether,

Tiphareth, Yesod and Malkuth. That on the left is named the Column of Severity, that on the right is the Column of Mercy; the central column is the Column of Equilibrium.

The Column of Severity being under the dominance of Binah is regarded as feminine: the Column of Mercy under Chokmah as masculine, and the Column of Equilibrium as bisexual or neutral.

Sometimes a student is bewildered to learn that the "feminine" column is that of Severity, not that of Mercy. It should be understood however that here we are dealing with principles, not with personalities. Further, the terms Mercy and Severity are convenient simplifications. The Column of Mercy represents giving and expansion; the Column of Severity represents reception and constriction.

The Column of Severity

In the order of emanation Binah receives the free and limitless energies from Chokmah and forms them, literally, into "concepts": whether as divine concepts, as mental concepts, as astral forms or as the shapes and structures of material being. In human life and learning "concepts" play an important part, reflecting strongly the maternal and formative functions of Binah. As an evident example, the child, after being subjected to the formative and constricting ambience of the womb, then experiences the formative influences of education and of training in the ways of his kindred. Similarly, in the course of education we are introduced to mathematical, philosophic, moral and other concepts, each limiting our processes of thought and at the same time directing them into channels of further development. As head of the Column of Severity, Binah transmits these qualities of restriction, education and re-formation to the Sephiroth below, Geburah and Hod.

The Severity of Geburah is more evident, for it aims at the forceful reshaping of what has already been formed: whether physically, by war, by surgery or by craftsman's decisive working of his material, or in the world of ideas where "reform" generally admits of no compromise. Geburah restores a state of justice, a reduction of excess when necessary: an earthquake or a volcanic eruption, correcting an imbalance of forces in the earth's crust, is as much a manifestation of Geburah as anything in human affairs.

In Hod, as in all the Sephiroth below Tiphareth, the picture is more subtle because it is more complex. This Sephirah is the true seat of magical knowledge and power. In a sense all knowledge is magical since it confers some degree of power: Hod is therefore the sphere of all knowledge and skills. But here too is constriction, for every subject of study, every skill, has its discipline, and the disciplines of Art Magic are multiple.

The austerity of Geburah is reflected in the exactitude and restraint of Hod, while the processes of analysis and crystallisation, also associated with Hod, more directly reflect aspects of the character of Binah.

The Column of Mercy

In contemplating the Sephiroth of the Column of Mercy, a change of feeling from the Column of Severity is at once perceptible. Here we are concerned with outgoing and unconditioned forces, in the Column of Severity with forces focused and directed to specific ends.

Chokmah, at the head of the Column of Mercy, is in Atziluth the power of the divine paternity. It comprises in potential the nature and power of all the other Sephiroth. As we contemplate it here, as not yet "conceptualised" by Binah, it is in a sense incomprehensible to us. To comprehend it fully, we should need to see its tremendous generative force, cosmic begetter of galaxies, of universes, united with an ideal paternal love and authority, justice and boundless generosity, all as one undivided whole.

The next Sephirah upon the Pillar of Mercy, Chesed, may be said to represent those qualities of Chokmah which, to the human mind, are the more recognisably paternal.

There is a patriarchal and priestly quality here, for a religious reverence as well as a filial love is evoked. The two titles of the Sephirah, Chesed and Gedulah, together express a boundless tenderness as well as a generosity born of the limitless power to give. The implication of these names is of an all-powerful justice making generous provision for each being: not as a measured reward for any good act or aspiration, but to give ample scope for present development and future progress. In this beneficent provision for future good, Chesed stands in balance with Geburah, the searching amender of past defect.

Of the Sephirah below Chesed upon the Column of Mercy — Netzach, sphere of the forces of nature — little need be said with regard to its qualities of liberality, vitality, joy. Netzach comes directly beneath the gentle beneficence of Chesed. But, again, here we move among the forces within the ambience of Tiphareth and the pattern becomes complex. As though to balance the seeming gentleness of Hod which stands opposite on the Pillar of Severity, the title of Netzach signifies "Victory". *Amor vincit omnia*; and the sweet and joyous forces of Netzach, carrying by the Way of Emanation the fire of the Sphere of the Sun, are in their own manner inexorable.

The Column of Equilibrium

The central column of the Tree of Life is not only considered as bisexual or neutral, nor yet simply as striking a balance between the forces of Severity and Mercy; it is in the human context the column of the mystic, of the seeker who looks into the shadows within to find the cosmic and eternal glories. Taken from the base upwards, it is in fact called the Path of the Mystic. That aspect of the matter is presented later in this book, but is mentioned now because of the special character of the Sephiroth which form this Column.

Kether, the head of this Column and source of the entire Tree, represents unconditioned divine power, and is totally outside ordinary perception or experience. Because it is the first Sephirah however, Kether receives in a special way those titles of God which express primordial being and unicity. Thus among its many other titles, Kether is the Single Light, the Most Holy Ancient One, Ancient of Days, the Head.

Kether is not in any exclusive sense "God". Qabalistically speaking, the whole World of Atziluth is "God". But to human consciousness in certain circumstances, the Sephirah Kether specially represents the hidden, unknowable, all-powerful glory of God.

That glory has however another representative which is more accessible to the imagination. This is the Sephirah Tiphareth.

Into Tiphareth, the sixth Sephirah, are gathered together the energic strength and the vital beneficence of Geburah and Chesed. By virtue of its position on the Tree, directly below Kether, Tiphareth also receives the infinite power of the primal divine purpose and manifests this in a mode comprehensible within the finite bounds of time and space. This mingled force then descends to the lower Sephiroth, adding something of the essential dynamism of Tiphareth to the particular character of each.

For this reason Joannes Rittangelius, in the renowned Qabalistic work "The Thirty-two Paths of Wisdom", says of Tiphareth:

The Sixth Path is the Intelligence of the mediatory influence. It is so named because into it is gathered the influx from all the Emanations, so that it in turn causes the mediatory influence to flow into the founts of all the benign powers, with which they are linked.

Tiphareth, on account of its position below Kether on the central column, is for us in a sense the representative of Kether, just as our Sun has been through the ages the acknowledged representative of the supernal glory.

Yesod, the ninth Sephirah, stands immediately below Tiphareth upon the central column of the Tree. It is the Sephirah nearest to Malkuth and we might say the most accessible to us; but its influence, conditioned by the Sephiroth above it, is the most multiform and the most difficult to interpret.

Yesod governs the astral world of dreams and visions, the true and the false, the lasting and the inconstant. The aspirant to magical knowledge and power, like the traveller in any new environment, must become inured to it, must find a passage through it without being overcome by either fear or fascination. There is a paradox, too, in the quality of Yesod: for the cold detachment which it receives from Hod on the way of emanation is countered by the reflection, on the Column of Equilibrium, of the fiery energy of Tiphareth.

The Sephirah Malkuth represents the forces of concretion and resolution. Its position at the foot of the central column — thus at the foot of the Tree — indicates that it receives, condenses and gives fruition to the influences of the nine other Sephiroth. Like each of them, Malkuth exists in all the four Worlds, and has its origin and primal reality in Atziluth. In each of the Worlds its forces are the same, their effects depending on the complexity of activity at that level.

For us, living in the Malkuth of Assiah, the powers and influences which are projected upon us spiritually, intellectually, emotionally, physically or in symbol, provide means to grow in awareness of the powers of all the Sephiroth, and in experience of the universe around us.

CHAPTER 8
THE WORDS OF POWER

Crowns of the Divine

The Qabalah ascribes to the Sephiroth particular biblical names, variously combined, to represent the character of the divine activity in the corresponding orders of being. Such names, referred to by the Zohar as "crowns", are the *Greater Words of Power* of the magical tradition,* the sacred mantra through which the godhead may be approached in contemplation and by which its power may be invoked. The Sephiroth are said to be "crowned" with these holy names.

In a more recondite image, the Zohar presents the Holy One himself, the Lord of the Universe, as adorned with multiple and diverse crowns of scintillant flame, these crowns being the same holy names, each established beyond time and space in the heights of Atziluth. So venerable a concept recalls the tradition that on each occasion when one of these names is reverently given forth, either vocally or by inscription of the Hebrew letters, the glory of the Holy One is thereby magnified.

The Greater Words of Power

KETHER — To the first Sephirah is ascribed the divine name **Ehyeh**: a formulation that implies unconditioned being, that betokens infinite "primordial light". In its longer form the name is **Ehyeh Asher Ehyeh**, rendered as "I am that which I am" and likewise conveying the concept of pure and unqualified being.

---

* The "Lesser Words of Power" are the names of the archangels of the World of Briah, and of the angels and angelic choras of the World of Yetzirah. See Part 4, tables 8, 10 and 11.

The Tetragrammaton, **YHVH**, is also assigned to Kether, but as a "hidden" attribution. It is not employed as a divine name for the first Sephirah, for it here represents the Holy One as he is in himself; not as he is subsequently revealed to us through his qualities made manifest in the processes of emanation.

CHOKMAH — The divine name is **Yah**. Being composed of the first two letters of the Tetragrammaton, this name properly signifies the union of Chokmah with Binah. The first letter, **Yod**, is particularly representative of Chokmah as the creative male principle, while the second letter, **Heh**, refers to the creative female principle Binah. The ascription of this name to the second Sephirah acknowledges a profound truth: that the unformed dynamism of Chokmah is perceptible to human consciousness not in itself, but only through the formative, conceptualising agency of Binah.

As "the Yod of Tetragrammaton", the divine force of Chokmah is pure dynamism, totally creative but essentially abstract and unformed.

Chokmah is also Abba**, "Father"**, a title of remote cosmic dignity, but representative none the less of a "Father of Lights" who may be approached in confidence, albeit with reverence, by his children of the lower Worlds.

BINAH — The divine name is **YHVH Elohim**. This formulation is called in the Zohar "the Perfect Name". It is said that when this name is uttered, the firmament is made resplendent with the glory of thirty-two lights. These lights are the Thirty-two Paths of the Tree of Life, and the name is thus seen to represent the fullness of supernal potential and energy concentrated within the creative ambience of the third Sephirah.

Equally valid as divine names here are **Elohim Chiim** ("the Living Elohim") and **Aima Elohim** ("Bright Mother Elohim"). Just as the force of Chokmah may be the better apprehended through its interaction with the third Sephirah, so Binah becomes intelligible through her reciprocity with the Father. Considered in isolation, Binah is **Ama**, "the dark Mother", constrictive and sterile. Impregnated by "the Yod of Tetragrammaton" she is **Aima**, "the bright Mother", who conceptualises and defines the unconditioned energies, the "Ideas", of the Father.

As head of the Column of Severity, Binah confers a particular quality upon the Sephiroth Geburah and Hod, and the word **Elohim** forms part of the divine names which express their nature.

CHESED — Receiving the influence of Chokmah on the Column of Mercy, Chesed interprets the power of the Supernal Father in terms of beneficent and just regard. For in the order of emanation, Chesed is also the first recipient of the divine power imbued with the qualities of the Supernal Mother. The divine name relating to the fourth Sephirah is **El**, "God", characterising a priestly king and celestial shepherd who is *pater familias*. The divine name **El Gedul**, meaning "the God of Glory" or "the High God", is also appropriately ascribed to this sphere.

GEBURAH — Situated below Binah on the Column of Severity, the fifth Sephirah bears the divine name **Elohim Gebor**, "the Elohim of Power, of Strength", "the Mighty God". The simple title **Elohim** is, however, appropriate here, and in the Zohar this is employed as the premier divine name of the sphere. Geburah is the antithesis or counterpoise of Chesed and, in the cosmic scheme, organises and defines the expansive and generous outpourings of the fourth Sephirah. Here, on the Column of Severity, the influence of Binah is felt again in its constrictive and formative aspect.

TIPHARETH — The sixth Sephirah, situated below Kether on the Column of Equilibrium, receives the influences of the Columns of Mercy and Severity and the vital force of supernal light. It thus unites and stabilises within itself all the sephirothic powers which have preceded it in the order of emanation. Within its ambience it holds, furthermore, the potential of Netzach, Hod, Yesod and Malkuth, into whose "founts" it channels the unified life-force in the further processes of emanation. It is, as the Zohar confirms, pre-eminently crowned with the divine name **YHVH**, whose mystery and splendour are here intelligibly disclosed.

The titles **Ha-Qadosh**, "the Holy One", and **Chai Aulomim**, "Life of the Worlds", are also particularly ascribed to the activity of the divine nature in the sixth Sephirah, expressing the dignity, the centrality and the unifying quality, of Tiphareth.

NETZACH — The seventh Sephirah has place below Chesed, on the Column of Mercy. As sphere of the forces of nature, Netzach is placed comprehensibly below that sphere which is associated with the influences of the heavens, and particularly with those benign forces which are represented in earthly symbolism by rain and dew.

Yet in order of emanation, Netzach is next after Tiphareth, and between Netzach and the glorious sixth Sephirah there exists a close relationship which is indicated in what almost seems an exchange of names. For Tiphareth is "Beauty" — a quality easily associated with Netzach as the sphere of natural life and love — and Netzach is "Victory", a quality belonging likewise to the mighty force of Tiphareth. The power and dignity of Netzach is not to be underestimated.

Thus it is that the divine name associated with Netzach is **YHVH Tzabaoth**: **YHVH** as continuing downwards that title which expresses the divine manifestation, and **Tzabaoth** to complete the glorious name of the God of Victory, "Lord of Hosts" — Lord of the hosts of heaven, Chief of all powers that be.

HOD — The eighth Sephirah, located below Geburah upon the Column of Severity, is next after Netzach in order of emanation. The premier divine name here is **Elohim Tzabaoth**: "the Elohim of Hosts", a title expressing mighty forces, not in manifestation but rather in the hidden functions of assimilation and of making anew. The creative and re-creative energies are not only carried to Hod from Binah through Geburah, but are reinforced by the mighty power of renewal which flows from Tiphareth, and by the indomitable life-force of Netzach. These forces are here crystallised by the intense and multifaceted power of Hod itself.

If Netzach is compared to the triumph of high summer as it ripens into harvest, then Hod may well be compared to the end of winter, as yet cold and silent, when the earth seems inert but in which the seeds swell towards germination, and the trees hold in their buds the promise of the leaves and blossoms of springtime. The divine title **Elohi Qedem** ("God of Old") is expressive of this aspect of Hod.

Hod is also the sphere of the transformative artist (whether working with words or with sounds or with other materials), the scientist, and in a most special way the alchemist. It is the sphere of all magic, and of all those who seek knowledge for the purpose of inner development and illumination. Very apposite here is the divine name **Elohim Emeth** ("God of Truth").

YESOD — In the ninth Sephirah the forces are gathered, directly from Tiphareth and from the Sephiroth below Tiphareth, and thus indirectly from the whole Tree. The immensity of the divine power focused in this Sephirah goes beyond imagery; and the main thrust of it - directly from Kether - is qualified only by the glory of Tiphareth.

The divine name associated with Yesod is **El Shaddai**. This is a venerable and most potent title, the name of the God of Abraham, Isaac and Jacob. It occurs in Genesis, in Exodus and in Ezekiel. The single name **Shaddai**, which is the form given in Numbers, Job, Ruth, and elsewhere in the bible, is likewise powerful and appropriate in this sphere.

The name **Shaddai** is so ancient that its exact meaning cannot be stated with certainty, but related words indicate that it alludes to the immense power of God. The Septuagint renders it into Greek as *Pantokrator*, the "All-Mover". **El Shaddai** has probably therefore been well perpetuated as "Almighty God", except that for many people the words have been worn so smooth in the vernacular by conventional usage that the full impact of their meaning is lost.

The divine name **El Chai** ("the Living God") is also attributed to Yesod. The glorious forces associated with every Sephirah are those of divine life: but the concentration of the divine forces and the magnitude of their action in Yesod inspire a particular reverence and wonder. In the Worlds of Yetzirah and Assiah — the two scarcely separable in this regard — we see the forces of Yesod most clearly and powerfully expressed in the functions of sexual love, of generation and birth. In the World of Briah, Yesod has a similar function in the fascination, the creative passion, the generation and bringing to birth of works of the mind. Many mystics, indeed, carry the Yesodic imagery of the lower Worlds further than this, for they seek to express their highest experiences without any other language to convey them but that of sexual passions and raptures. Yet even that failure of articulation may suggest something to us of the intense vitality of the Yesod of Atziluth.

MALKUTH — It is clear from the Zohar that the divine name essentially associated with the tenth Sephirah is simply **Adonai**, a title of God in scriptural usage in its own right, meaning "Lord". Sometimes the Zohar even gives this title to the Shekinah,* that wondrous female manifestation of the divine presence in Malkuth which, whether felt or perceived as a radiance, has in certain times and places been discerned by souls that were harmonious to her.

This divine name is also associated with Malkuth in amplified forms. **Adonai Melekh**, "Lord and King", declares the divine rulership of the Sephirah Malkuth, the cosmic splendour and authority of the Holy One. **Adonai ha-Aretz**, "Lord of the World", has reference to God as Lord and Guardian of the physical world itself.

A further formulation appropriate to Malkuth is the superb and emphatic **Adon kol ha-Aretz**, "Lord of the whole World", which is to be found in the Book of Joshua.

---

* The Zoharic attribution is not so strange as it may at first appear for, as with the aspects of deity in every Sephirah, the Shekinah participates in the nature of the One Supreme. And besides, members of the cosmopolitan mediaeval culture of Spain will not have been unaware that the troubadours of Provence often gave the title of *Seigneur*, "Lord", to the lady of their earthly adoration. The mystics of the Zohar could not do less than accord this title to her to whom it eminently belonged.

Part 2
THE WORLDS OF THE FALLIBLE AND THE NATURE OF MAN

CHAPTER 9
THE QLIPPOTH

Good and evil: a practical view

Aristotle, a pupil of Plato, shared in many of the insights of his master, although the field of his enquiries was, in general, less abstract than that of Plato. Among numerous other philosophic concerns, he was interested in the nature and function in human life of the pursuit of goodness — which included both virtue and happiness — and the avoidance of evil. When Aristotle says, "The good is that at which all things aim," he is certainly assenting to the philosophic doctrine that the goal of all existences is union with the Supreme Good; but his more immediate concern is with the concept that all human action, no matter how foolish or misguided, is in intention directed to the better quality of life, and therefore the greater happiness of the doer.

However, because Aristotle's views concerning human behaviour are based, essentially and sincerely, upon an unquestioning assumption of the underlying spiritual values, we can look as it were through his observations on human life in a small city-state to the cosmic perspectives beyond: much as we can see the archetypes behind the characters which a great playwright sets upon the stage to portray the specific aspirations and deficiencies of his own era.

A philosophy of action

Three main points emerge from a consideration of Aristotle's ethics: main points in context of the present study, but fundamental also to a fair assessment of the work of the philosopher. One is the fact that in Aristotle's view it is necessary that a good quality should be cultivated by the avoidance both of its deficiency and of its excess. A second point is that cultivation of the good is to be achieved through positively right action (which, clearly, can include speech and even active thought), not through a mere avoidance of wrong action.

For instance, a man does not cultivate courage merely by avoiding both cowardly action and foolhardiness: he has to act with boldness combined with prudence. So with liberality: one must act with liberality to give reality to the fact that one is neither parsimonious nor prodigal.

The third point — and for us the most important to observe in Aristotle's treatment of the subject — is that all of the human qualities which he considers are, or would be in their right context and proportions, virtues. Those qualities which become vices do so, not because of any intrinsic evil within themselves, but through being, in their specific action and manifestation, out of equilibrium with other virtues.

Such qualities do not become evil in their intrinsic nature. They cannot. As Plato would put it, the *Ideas* of valour or of good husbandry, of justice or of sexual love, cannot become evil. But when any quality becomes inordinate in relation to other qualities, then it becomes a vice, resulting in wrong action and distorted character.

Excellence, not fanaticism

The practical ethics of Aristotle do not consitute a defence of mediocrity. Without doubt his outlook reflects the general Athenian attitude of avoidance of extremes; but, equally without doubt, that attitude did not deter the philosophers, the dramatists or the legists, the architects, the sculptors or the athletes of Athens from striving for excellence, each in his own field.

What Aristotle advocates is precisely the attitude which was set forth by Pericles in his funeral oration, 404 BC, for the Athenians fallen in the Peloponnesian war. As recorded at that time by the historian Thucydides, Pericles' words included this memorable passage:

"We love beauty without becoming luxurious, we love wisdom without becoming weak. Riches are not to us merely a matter for boasting, but a means to be used towards attainment; nor do we consider it shameful to confess to poverty, although we would think it truly disgraceful not to try to remedy it. In Athens everyone takes care, not only of his private duties but in public concerns, so that even those who must give most attention to their personal business do not let it stand in the way of their knowing thoroughly that of the city ...... We are outstanding as being most forthright in action, but the dangers we face are calculated beforehand." *(History of the Peloponnesian War,* II.40)

The implications

Aristotle's reasoned evaluation of human conduct is significant to us, in that it demonstrates a source of moral defect — even of iniquity — which corresponds to general experience and which requires no explanation dependent upon any theological dualism. Every quality involved in this philosophy is good in its primal nature; it may become evil by becoming inordinate, and it may become a cause of other and greater evils; but the root of these evils, and of all evil, is imbalance, whether through a sane but improper choice or through an imbalance within the person. Indeed, when we speak of injustice — which can be monstrous — and of iniquity — which can reach the blackest depths but which, by analysis, is "in-equity" — we can perceive how far-reaching in truth is this perception of Aristotle's.

While we may say, however, that imbalance is the root of all evil, it would be neither logical nor in accord with the facts to say that all imbalance is in itself evil. Life proceeds from one imbalance to another, whether we consider the life of an individual person or the life of the earth generally. Humanly, we can judge an occurrence to be "good" or "bad" according to its circumstances and effects, but this is a very different matter from the experience of true evil. True evil is unbalanced force thrust to a pernicious extreme, with the presence in that force of some degree, however blind, of volition.

Perceiving true evil to be inseparable from willed harm, it can be seen that the simple imbalances which present themselves in the ordinary current of events cannot reasonably be identified as "evil", inconvenient or painful though their experience may be. Even such catclysmic events as flood and earthquake, hurricane and volcanic eruption, are but violent restorations of equilibrium to imbalances which had built up in the natural order. As the change and progression of the seasons produces the harvests, so one and another challenge of circumstances produces stimulus and impetus in life. Falling in love, for instance, can hardly be described as an "evil", although it is certainly a state of imbalance and can be disastrous in the wrong circumstances; most frequently, of course, the forces involved are soon happily equilibrated. To take an ecological example, a fire in forest or heathland is generally seen as calamitous, and yet there are some plants — the beautiful golden gorse is the most common example — which thrive the better as a result of it.

In what follows concerning unbalanced forces with their first origins, something far other and deeper is to be treated of, than the small or great imbalances which daily come into being, manifest themselves, and are by one means or another brought into a new balance, in the normal course of existence. The unbalanced forces here treated of are termed the Qlippoth. Originating from the primal cosmic order, they are yet alien to all cosmic order and unity. They are in themselves extremes of unbalanced force, and are thus focal points for other unbalanced forces including the most intense concentrations of psychic evil. From this point however, the nature of the Qlippoth and the causes of their existence need to be set forth in terms of Qabalistic teaching.

Primal imbalances

The first and inevitable question is, How was it possible for imbalance, excessive imbalance, to arise in the primal order?

The classic explanation has an apparent simplicity which can be somewhat misleading. It is that in the course of the emanation of the Sephiroth — as exemplified by the pattern of the Lightning Flash — when each new Sephirah in its turn was in a state of unbalanced profusion until brought into equilibrium by the emanation of the next Sephirah, the overplus of energy which it threw off became qlippothic.

As regards the Worlds below Atziluth, this general statement of the emergence of the Qlippoth is valid. *It cannot be applied however to the primal emanation of the Sephiroth within Atziluth,* for it presents the process of emanation as entirely a temporal phenomenon, occupying time however briefly. It presumes a moment, even if only an infinitesimal moment, between the emanations of Sephirah and Sephirah, for the emergence of the Qlippoth. *On this basis alone, were there no other, the origin of the Qlippoth could not be imputed to the World of Atziluth the divine World which exists wholly apart from time.* The injury to the divine unity and integrity which would be supposed by such an imputation is another sufficient reason for rejecting it.

It would also militate against that luminous concept which is essential to the development of Qabalistic teaching: the concept of the divine attributes formulated into the ten Sephiroth, and these into the perfect Tree of Life, within the Divine Mind as a preliminary to the communication of the sephirothic forces to the lower Worlds. For this concept of the Tree, whole and integrated within the Divine Mind, is perceived as within the ambience of eternity; and eternity, properly understood, is not a name given to unending time but is a mode of being into which time does not enter.

However, this does not invalidate the concept of the Sephiroth having thrown off the qlippothic forces as they emanated in the lower Worlds. The Sephiroth in Atziluth belong to a wholly different order of being from their manifestations in the Worlds of Briah, Yetzirah and Assiah, where the conditions of time obtain.

It is in these latter conditions that the Qlippoth have come into being and exercise their influence. There are no Qlippoth of the World of Atziluth.

The great defect in the Qlippoth

In the teeming plenitude of life in the universe — not only "life as we know it", to use a phrase beloved by the scientists, but life of all conceivable and inconceivable kinds — it can readily be accepted that there is no mode of existence which is not represented by living or quasi-living entities. Thus it is with the qlippothic modes of existence, primarily inert forces, each with its aggregated impulsions or entities, its specific "tribe" of Qlippoth.

It may be asked why in so wide and varied a universe of life these particular entities, the Qlippoth, should be identified as distinctively inimical, beyond the capacity for harm of any bacterial or viral agency, beyond that of any inanimate forces such as lightning or whirlwind, beyond that of any sheer negation such as polar cold. Any of these may indeed become at one time or another excessive, but they are not therefore qlippothic. The case of the Qlippoth is altogether singular.

It is as regards their link with their sephirothic archetype in the Divine Mind that the Qlippoth are in dereliction. As forces dissociated from their Sephirah they lack that link; and thus they lack also the vital effects of the communication of that archetype with every other in the Divine Mind, the highest level of unity of all existences. That is precisely why they are named *Qlippoth*, for the word means "shells". Instead of their particular nature being infused with the spiritual light, life and purpose of the World of Atziluth, which would make them participants in the Divine Plan, they remain dark and empty, engrossed to obsession in the preservation and magnification of their own nature.

They are capable of preying on the energies of other beings, and of absorbing whatever Yetziratic and Assiatic forces they can seize upon; but they cannot appease their continual hunger for the Atziluthic life which they lack, and which every normal living being receives in its own measure, whether consciously or not. The Qlippoth, unable in any circumstances to obtain this higher life, impelled as they are by hunger for it and infused with malice, conceive an extreme jealousy and an implacable hostility against the living participants of the entire cosmos.

Any sufferings they may inflict are to them merely a means of obtaining energic nourishment: to serve the same purpose they will contrive pleasure with equal unconcern, but the gift of real joy or happiness is beyond both their power and their interest.

Integration

In this changeful and far-from-ideal world, forces in one aspect of existence or another often go out of balance. Usually, whether in the natural order or in human affairs, the unbalanced force is soon equilibrated and there is little we need to do. Occasionally the process of equilibration is cataclysmic and there is little we can do. Seldom is there need to suspect the intervention of more than natural or human activity.

On rare occasions, however, the experienced occultist meets with examples of obsessive influences, of malign hauntings not of the human kind, which show themselves as unmistakably qlippothic. To deal effectively with such manifestations, skilled magical action is required.

A qlippothic force cannot as such be equilibrated with normal forces: it must first be normalised by integration to its sephirothic archetype. To this end, the integrating power must be drawn from the archetypal level in the World of Atziluth. The work may be undertaken in the ambience of the external cosmos or — more surely, given the knowledge, the inner power and the daring — by assimilation of the qlippothic force to the archetypal power, within the psyche of the magician. This having been effected, any excess of force is now within the natural order and may be equilibrated by normal magical process.

The entire action, especially when the integration of the qlippothic force is conducted within the psyche of the operator, is one which calls for a degree of perspicacity, experience of occult forces, and spiritual integrity which cannot be minimised, and which makes this operation not only a paramount work of the Light but a major magical challenge.

CHAPTER 10
HUMANKIND, EARTHLY AND ARCHETYPAL

A marginal note

The Supernal Man of Qabalistic tradition is frequently referred to as *Adam Qadmon*. The second part of this name, QDMVN, means "primaeval" or "prototypic". Thus the name can rightly be rendered, "Archetypal Man".

A curious comment on the subject of the Archetypal Man may set in a clear light some of the points which need to be unravelled. Charles Kingsley, clergyman, novelist and poet in the nineteenth century, was something of an original thinker. His novel *Hypatia* tells with perception and sympathy the story of a notable woman of the Greek culture of Alexandria who met a tragic death in the year 415 of this era. She was a writer upon astronomy and mathematics, she took pupils in philosophy and is said to have lectured upon that subject. Her great desire was to create and to maintain a state of society based upon the noblest aspirations of Plato and Aristotle.

In one episode of Kingsley's story, a Christian friend tries to interest her in his religion. He asks her, "Have you ever considered what the Idea of Man might be like?" — and after a little, giving his own thoughts on this theme, he says "It is possible to imagine a man who is not a father, but it is not possible to imagine a man who is not a son." To be a son is seen as an essential quality of the prototypic representative of humanity.

Certainly we can presume that a man of Kingsley's era and education knew his *Poimandres*, and would have perceived the close relationship of its thought to that of the opening passage of the Gospel of John. But his direct pointing to the heart of this knot of conceptual reasoning is noteworthy.

"Let us make Man ..."

We turn now to consider a passage of the Zoharic commentary on Genesis which purports to record the discourse of one Rabbi Simeon. There may be some question as to what scriptural version is the basis of this discourse, but most likely it is simply an interpretation made by combining the two accounts of the creation of man as we have them in Genesis: the *"Elohim"* version in chapter 1 and the *"YHVH Elohim"* version in chapter 2.

This apparent combination of texts becomes however in the Zohar the point of departure for a significant interpretation of the creation of man in terms of a dialogue between YHVH and Elohim.

A definite (though mythic) theological reason for this interpretation is produced: the Father, it is said, hesitated to participate in the making of man, so the bringing into being of humankind — at least of the manifestation of humankind in the lower Worlds — remained altogether the responsibility of the Mother.

It is interesting to follow the argument of the Zoharic writer in making this interpretation. He likens the Father to a king who desires to have some building work done, and the Mother to the king's architect. In the ideal World of Atziluth all goes harmoniously. In the lower Worlds however, when the Mother proposes the making of Man as a created being with a real existence in those Worlds, the Father demurs. As a created being, the Father declares, Man will commit sin as a result of fallibility; he will be the "foolish son" (BN KSIL) of Proverbs who is a burden to his mother, as contrasted with the "wise son" (BN ChKM), Supernal Man, who brings joy to his father. It is at that point that the Mother assumes all responsibility for created man and his future guilt, and he is accordingly created "in the image of Elohim". In consequence, just as the Mother has both a dark and a bright aspect, so man too is a creature of darkness and also of light.

Although there is far more to be said concerning incarnate humanity than can be included in this chapter — incarnate humanity, and particularly the incarnate mage, being the main subject of the rest of this book — nevertheless a preliminary glance at that theme, suggested by the narrative from the Zohar which is outlined above, has a rightful place at this juncture.

The Tree and the Worlds

When we come to consider the Tree of Life from the viewpoint of human experience rather than objective cosmic reality, there is another formulation which will be presented besides those given earlier in this book: the **Composite Tree**, in which the experience of certain Sephiroth is linked to certain of the Four Worlds. That is by no means a new formulation; the older writers often take it for granted to the extent that they do not seem to notice any singularity in it. It is as if a person living in a large house were to forget the existence of the rooms which lie behind the staircase.

The view of the Tree which should be noticed at present is less complex, and seems to be peculiar to Zoharic texts. While it is recognised that the Tree exists whole and entire in Atziluth — the "World of Emanations" — in considering the descent of the Sephiroth through the Worlds there is a tendency to disregard the presence of the Supernals in the lower Worlds, and also to group together Briah, Yetzirah and Assiah as the "Worlds of Manifestation". Consequently Kether, Chokmah and Binah are conceived of as remaining in the World of Atziluth, while all the Sephiroth below Binah are together regarded as existing in the collective "Worlds of Manifestation".

This formulation is admissible provided that its employment is recognised, otherwise it could cause confusion of thought for the student. In reflecting upon the Zoharic narrative given above, it helps to clarify the special function of Binah in relation to the Worlds of Manifestation, and thus to show also the complete distinction between Supernal Man and his earthly counterpart.

The work of Binah

Binah stands at the threshold of the Worlds of Manifestation, for they are her work. She has not only gathered from the other Supernals the energies which go to making the fabric of the universe, she has added her own store.

The World of Mind, Briah, is the most subtle, yet the most spiritually potent of the Worlds of Manifestation, while the Causal World, Yetzirah, brings a denser web of inwoven energies almost to materialisation. These energies merge with no line of demarcation into the radiation and electrical forces of Assiah, the material World.

Having completed the downward emanation, she **has created**: spinning and interweaving those energies into the patterns of (as we should say nowadays) proton, neutron and electron, of atom and molecule, of gas, vapour, liquid and solid stuff, of blood, bone and muscle; she has woven the fine web of mind and the denser web of feeling, she has formed the constellations and the planets and attuned their influences to the divine qualities they are severally destined to carry. And, these once formulated, the influences of condensation, solidification and crystallisation — qualities which we term Saturnian — come into play to confirm the work.

Into all this pulsating universe of light and colour, of music heard and unheard and into the bewildering custody of mind, soul and body, man descended as a created and fallible being. It is for this reason that the Mother declared that since the Father would not take responsibility for him she would make man in her own likeness. **He shall be my care**, she states, and her declaration in its full implication signifies: **he shall be a being of light and darkness, even as he has body, soul and mind as well as the supernal spirit: he may fall, but because of his very complexity he shall be able to arise again.***

The "wise son" in Atziluth

Turning now to the subject of the "wise son", the Supernal Man, certain points are clearly intended to be gathered from the passage in the Zohar which is considered earlier in Chapter 4.

The Supernal Man became "a chariot" by which the Holy One became manifest in the lower Worlds in his name YHVH. Out

---

* This is due to the nature, not only of man but also of the Mother. Among the names of Binah is that of Ama (AMA) which signifies the Mother in her dark and sterile aspect. The name Aima (AYMA), however, signifies the Mother as luminous and fertile, because the *Yod* (Y) which has been added signifies the generative power of the Father. But clearly the name Aima always contains the name Ama: from which we may conclude that the Mother as Aima is at once sterile and fertile, at once dark and luminous. So she receives kindly the fallible son of darkness, then opens for him the way to the light.

of this four other inferences arise:

(a) The Holy One descends — that is, his presence becomes recognised — in this "chariot" through the Four Worlds, which correspond to the letters YHVH.

(b) Since the Holy One cannot in his inner nature be perceived by us, but only meet our awareness by certain qualities, the "chariot" must be a manifestation of these qualities and, more clearly to us, of his attributes. For, as he is Truth, nothing except his own qualities and attributes can indicate his presence.

(c) Although we on earth are represented by the created, the "foolish son", nevertheless the Supernal Man is our archetype and therefore our inner being is able to respond — indeed to correspond — albeit in its unconscious depths, to this manifestation of the divine.

(d) When this is considered in conjunction with the manifestation of the Holy One through the Worlds by his qualities and attributes, the Three and the Seven, the "chariot" can at once be identified as the Tree of Life, the Ten Sephiroth which, as we have seen, bring down their own manifestations through the Worlds. Moreover, the formulation of the Tree of Life is identified with that of the Supernal Man in Atziluth, who has a unique relationship to humankind in the lower Worlds. This brings us close to the conclusion of the present line of exploration.

Supernal Man and the Tree of Life

The Supernal Man does not come into incarnation. He is, properly speaking, the "archetype of humanity" rather than "archetypal man", for this formulation of the divine attributes is not shaped in any human likeness. **An archetype has no image**.

The theology of the ancient Hebrew scriptures accords upon this point with the findings of Carl Jung, who, it must be remembered, took every care to base his statements entirely upon his certainties as physician and psychologist. No archetype in its simple essence, whether discerned in the heights of divine light — in the World of Atziluth as we should say — or in the deeps of the Collective Unconscious, has any image. The human psyche, upon becoming aware of an archetypal presence, will spontaneously clothe it — as in the dreaming state — with whatever form that psyche finds suitable. Thus an archetypal image is formed, but it is not integral to the archetype.

This is true, of course, not only of any human shape in which we might figure to ourselves the archetype of humanity. It is true also of the diagrammatic form in which we constantly represent the Tree of Life. The divine attributes do not manifest themselves as ten circles neatly arranged; that, however revered, is a formulation made by the human mind to render intelligible the inter-relationship of the divine attributes.

Our Way of Aspiration

None the less, it is true that the Tree of Life as we have it does show forth certain essential qualities of the archetype of humanity. It is "bisexual" in that the Pillar of Mercy is considered as male in quality, the Pillar of Severity as female; besides this, every Sephirah of whatever attribution is considered male to the Sephirah below it, female to the Sephirah above. (Kether on this account is considered all-male, Malkuth all-female; which gives polarity to the Central Column.) As the archetype of humanity it thus represents man and woman impartially, since each person manifests — in psyche and in body — one sex in a developed, the other in a recessive state.

It is tempting, certainly, at this point to look at the diagram of the Tree (as it has been formulated on earth) and to reflect, It has a left side and a right side, a central spine, a foot, a head — perhaps after all it is the conventionalised form of a human person. But beware! You do not have your head in Kether, not even in your own personal Kether. And the Tree represents you in a more subtle way than you may think.

The Tree is the diagram of that nucleus of yourself, the perfect Idea of yourself in the Divine Mind; that to which your aspiration will turn. The Tree also represents your whole potential, extending as it does through the regions of physical being and of emotion, of intellectual thought and — in its true development — of intuition, of your unification with your Higher Self which is a true part of the Divine Mind.

The Tree of Life shows the full scope of development of your nature, up to the magical and mystical heights. *Properly understood, it is also the map which will guide you on that road.* Although we begin by being identified with the "foolish son", the upward way is open.

CHAPTER 11
THE POWERS WITHIN US

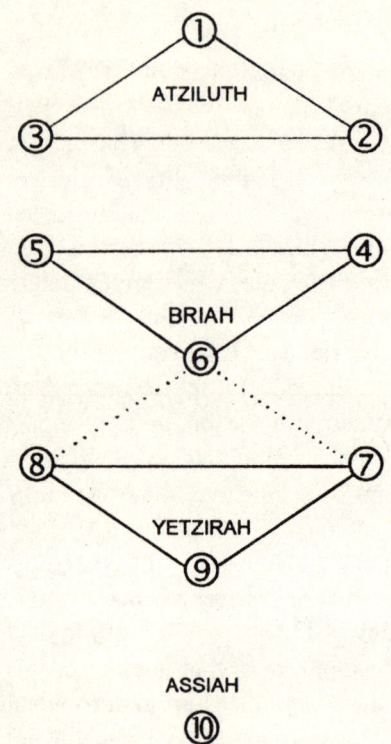

The functions of the psyche

The Pythagoreans recognised four levels within the psyche: in ascending order, these were the perceptive, imaginative, rational and intuitive levels. That classification has, in its essentials, never been bettered. In the Zohar the levels or functions of the psyche are set forth in terms which show a close agreement with the Pythagorean classification, if we refer the Pythagorean "perceptive level" to the sense-perceptions of the physical body.

The Nephesh, the "lower soul", comprises the nerve impulses which unite psyche and body, the simple interpretation of those impulses, the instincts both unconscious and conscious and the emotions up to the most elevated.

The Ruach, the mind or "higher soul", is initially simply the rational mind, having the function of examining the evidence of the senses as conditioned by the Nephesh (this including the results of every mode of learning), making deductions from them or bringing in other evidence in consideration of a hypothesis. The Ruach is described by the Zohar as being seated upon the Nephesh as upon a throne; but the Nephesh is apt to present its material to the Ruach with various kinds of emotional and instinctual bias, even of bias due to physical conditions, and if the Ruach is untrained, or yields habitually to the Nephesh, the judgment can be swayed thereby and perhaps disastrously. All will be well, however, if the Ruach learns to form its own rational decisions without thereby suppressing the imaginative faculty of the Nephesh.

When a right relationship exists between Nephesh and Ruach in the full and normal development of the psyche, the action of a third factor, the Neshamah, in due course reveals itself. The Neshamah is the supreme directing influence of the psyche, and as such now comes gradually into prominence.

The term "Neshamah" can be, and often is, used to signify the entire spiritual pinnacle, so to call it, of our inner structure: that is, to signify an area corresponding to Binah, Chokmah and Kether on the cosmic Tree. With this connotation the term "Neshamah" should more exactly be "triune Neshamah". For, where an exact analysis is needed, each of the three supernal functions within the psyche is distinctly identified. The Neshamah strictly so called corresponds to the function of Binah within us, the function of Chokmah is represented by the **Chiah**, and the **Yechidah** is the microcosmic representative of Kether.

The Psyche, the Worlds, the Sephiroth

As is set forth in Chapter 4, the Four Worlds of the exterior universe have their counterparts within us, the physical body being of the substance of the World of Assiah, the Nephesh of the World of Yetzirah, the Ruach of the World of Briah and the triune Neshamah of the World of Atziluth. **It is therefore by the progressive realisation and illumination of our own natural faculties, in their respective areas and rightful order, that our spiritual evolution takes place.**

We have seen in Chapter 10 that Supernal Man, our archetype, is of one Atziluthic formulation with the Tree of Life comprising the ten Sephiroth. In each person that archetype is present, a living potentiality to be gloriously realized. How then is our inner ascent of the Worlds by way of the Sephiroth to be interpreted?

The Composite Tree

A brief mention has been made of the Composite Tree. This is a microcosmic formulation which has a particular relevance to the Way of Return, and in much of the earlier literature of the Qabalah its existence and function are taken for granted without its being accorded an explicit description.

The diagram of the Composite Tree at the beginning of this chapter shows the relationship of the Worlds to the Sephiroth on the Way of Return, an ascent by way of the Sephiroth and the Worlds simultaneously being uniformly assumed by the earlier Qabalistic writers. The implied ascent through the Worlds signifies certainly an inner progress from one operative level of the psyche to the next; but since not only steady development but a decisive further awakening of the sephirothic powers in the psyche is envisaged, the allocation of certain of the Sephiroth to specific functions is less rigidly defined.

The diagram also shows that the Sephiroth of the Composite Tree, apart from Malkuth, are grouped in three triads. These offer much material for reflection in their correspondence both to the functions of the psyche and to the Worlds, and can be summarised thus:

Malkuth — physical body — World of Assiah;
Yesod, Hod, Netzach — astral body — World of Yetzirah;
Tiphareth, Geburah, Chesed — mental sheath — World of Briah;

Binah, Chokmah, Kether — spirit — World of Atziluth.

The indicated ascent is an exact system, with defined points, the "Gates", at which alone a transition of consciousness from World to World can be made. These Gates to the Worlds, with the Sephiroth to which they give access and the corresponding levels of the psyche, are next to be considered.

The First Gate: Malkuth into Assiah

This is the World and the sphere into which we are born, the end of our descent into incarnation. In fact, "The Gate" is one of the recognised titles of Malkuth, and to the World of Assiah is ascribed the physical body. However, every magician, with every poet, prophet and mystic, finds early in life that the Nephesh, lacking at first the full exercise of its faculties in Yetzirah, feasts avidly upon all the beauty and wonder, psychic nurture and stimulation, to be found in the visible world. The Malkuth of Assiah is thus truly the first Gate, not only bringing us into incarnation but placing us on the threshold, and letting us glimpse the invitation, of other Worlds to which we are also native.

The Second Gate: Yesod into Yetzirah

Led by dream and daydream and by the growing faculties of the psyche, the Nephesh discovers its heritage in the World of Yetzirah, where at first it scarcely realizes its own passage from one level of being to another.

There it makes its playground, and will be the passive recipient of many and varied impressions. It cannot however explore with full purpose or move with authority therein, until it has gained its magical entrance to the Sephirah Yesod and has experienced, and assimilated, the bewildering power of that Sphere. When that is accomplished, the Nephesh is able to enter into the Sephiroth of Hod and Netzach *at their Yetziratic levels,* and to direct its action therein.

All this activity will be that of the Nephesh in its natural World. However intently, all is done in play. There can be strong emotions, vivid imagination, experiences that will linger in the memory, but here there can be no moral responsibility, no true act of the will;

and this is equally the case, whether we speak of the fantasies of a young child at play or the dreams of a sleeping adult. In such cases, it is recognised, the Nephesh can manifest itself according only to its own nature, its one law being that of self-expression. It is otherwise when a person who should be in a higher state of consciousness and of responsibility is so entranced by the scientific or magical potential of Hod, or by the overpowering vital force of Netzach, as to leave adult judgment and treat life-and-death matters as toys. But, looking to adult judgment, we look to a function of the psyche above the Nephesh.

The Third Gate: Tiphareth into Briah

In the normal development of the psyche the powers of the Ruach — the mental faculty which functions at the Briatic level — are active at an early but variable age, although the "age of reason" is conventionally set at seven years. In what follows however we refer to the awakening of the Ruach to a more advanced degree of consciousness, one which is in no way related to physical age: the opening to the consciousness of the World of Briah by entrance into the Sphere of Tiphareth. Whether this entrance is made by means of ritual action, through inward aspiration or through some other signal experience of life, to make it is to be initiated, with or without full realisation, to the commitments and high splendours of the Way of adepthood. This attainment may indeed have been precipitated, and its experiences intensified, by one or other of the means above suggested, but it must be understood that it is in itself but the rightful completion of human nature, the crowning of the psyche — and thus of the whole personality — with the fullness of its powers. No matter how it may have come about, however, the initiate in the World of Briah is not likely at once to perceive the extent and depth of the change in outlook, and of the psychic ambience, which has taken place.

Primarily, as we have seen, the Ruach has by nature the responsibility of governing the Nephesh and the physical body, not harshly but with benign reason. Beyond this, it is the decision-making faculty of the whole personality; and these are responsibilities which it cannot escape.

The Sephiroth which are now opened to it in their plenitude are, besides Tiphareth itself, the great governing spheres of Geburah and Chesed and, as indicated by the dotted lines in our diagram, the Briatic levels of Hod and Netzach. These last two, besides the simple enjoyment and wonder of the Nephesh, can now be accorded by the Ruach their rightful appreciation.

The development of the Ruach itself is, however, to be regarded. Of its primal nature, the Ruach works by logical processes of reasoning, based upon such knowledge as it can acquire from whatever source. But sources of knowledge may be at fault. The Nephesh, or some bodily condition, may also induce error. Moreover the Ruach, even if these processes of conscious reasoning were flawless, is not designed to be wholly dependent upon them in fulfilling its position in the psyche.

Now, as it opens more and more fully to its true Briatic consciousness, the Ruach has a greater comprehension of itself as well as of the mental ambience in which it functions. Stage by stage it grows away from the familiar images, accepted phrases, preconceived ideas, which have often taken the place of true thought. New perceptions of reality take their place, with a freshness and certainty of cognition which is a continual source of joy: a joy not lessened by being mingled with a deep earnestness. The growing adept mentally explores all the Briatic spheres, absorbing and experiencing their qualities, but with an increasing consciousness of the need to advance yet further. How, for example, is he to direct with right discretion and in due circumstances the great faculties of Strength and of Mercy in his psyche, without exercising some power of discernment higher even than they?

At the same time, as he advances, he has an ever surer realisation that he is not in fact left unaided. The Ruach, central to the personality as Tiphareth is central to the Tree, is situated not only to govern those functions which are within its own World but to be receptive to those which are above it. Scarcely perceived at first but growing in the awareness of the recipient, a beam from the triune Neshamah strikes through the still unrevealed gate of Daath to illumine and fortify the Ruach; an increasing contact of the **Intuitive Mind**, to bring the faculties of the Ruach in due course to their rightful completion.

Yet a description in these terms makes a cold and impersonal matter of a profoundly personal experience, of the increasing certainty of the presence of a true friend and companion upon the Way. The mode of this certainty varies, indeed, from person to person, but it admits of no doubt. Besides this, and as surely, there are portions of knowledge imparted, not by the accustomed means nor by any communication from external discarnate entities, but by a simple inner awareness rather like the spontaneous recalling of something long since known but forgotten. These illuminations are the work of the Intuitive Mind, which is a beam from the Yechidah transmitted through the Neshamah, and which manifests intelligibly as the mysterious Presence for which a form may or may not be imagined: the adept's Holy Guardian, or Higher Self, or Divine Friend —

Not in the ordinary sense "self", but that divine being with whom one will ultimately become united, or rather reunited: that primal concept in the Divine Mind, luminous and living, the true "self" which is one's ideal pattern, with whom one is destined to be indissolubly *one;* the glorious Being who truly loves one — this is the marvel — not for one's poor merits but because one is oneself, the unique earthly counterpart of that Being who is —

Not "God" in the sense of the One Most Holy, the Lord of the Universe, the Maker of the Worlds, for to be one in identity with that One were impossible although some mystics have not seen the distinction: but "God" in the sense that this Being is in full verity a spark of, is wholly one with, the divine nature in Atziluth, and no matter how many million such sparks there may be in the Mind of the Eternal, each spark is as truly divine as is the Mind by which it is emanated and from which it has never been sundered —

Not infinite in nature, this spark, for no matter how glorious in light and beauty, it is conceived as the True Self of a human creature. But not "finite" in knowledge, nor in power of life and of love. For each of these sparks in Atziluth is linked in one splendour of knowledge, of life, of love and of power with every other such spark, and directly too with the Divine Mind which enwraps the universe; so that the individual self of the adept, when united to the particular spark which is the concept and nucleus of its own origin, will be in entire communication with all of these glories.

Before this ecstasy can be brought to entire realisation however, there is an ordeal to be passed.

The Fourth Gate: Daath into Atziluth

To pass from the World of Briah, even from its heights, into the World of Divinity is not easy of achievement. In cold reason, nobody would attempt it; but in whatever field of high endeavour, it is the inspiration of the Intuitive Mind, and the courage to accept it, which leaves cold reason far behind and distinguishes the attainment of the genius from that of the proficient.

Our adept, to enter spiritually the World of Atziluth, must pass from the world of Briah to Supernal Binah; and must to this end first traverse, by the gate of Daath, in inner experience, that gulf between the Briatic and the Atziluthic modes of being which is frequently called the Abyss.

When illustrated diagrammatically, Daath is set on the central column of the Tree as are the other gates between the Worlds, and immediately below the supernal Sephiroth. It is not however a Sephirah, for it has no place in the primal order of emanation of the Sephiroth. It is not an objective mode of being; it represents an inner reality of the psyche which is of supreme importance in relation to the Way of Return. In relating Daath to the spiritual life, its nature can be more easily expressed in terms of the Worlds than of the Sephiroth, for it is for the psyche a necessary phase of transition from the consciousness of Briah to that of Atziluth, a dynamic interaction between the Intuitive Mind and the Ruach. Before the actual transition is made, perhaps long before, this interaction has been active in those impulses of the Intuitive Mind of which the adept has become conscious; active, too, in the presence and in the guiding companionship of the Holy Guardian. Thus in this living ambience of spiritual light and love, growing progressively more aware of the higher faculties, the adept is drawn to the fulfilment and spiritual completion of his human nature. This progression however, whatever the time-span of its achievement, leads inevitably to that unique inner experience which is the fullness of Daath. For Daath is Knowledge, which is *Gnosis*, a life-transforming instant of divine illumination to the psyche: and it is in this illumination, and the willed acceptance of it, that the Abyss is passed.

Predictably, the bright Being on whom the adept has learned to rely, his Divine Friend and Holy Guardian, will at this critical time seem to have retired from his consciousness. *The age-old recounting of the experience is ever thus.* But a beam of invisible light from the Intuitive Mind will show, so to put it, the onward way. Drawn by a compulsion to fulfil his destiny at all costs, and to hazard the loss of all to win the only hope of regaining all, the adept presses forward to the greatest transition which can be made by one who remains incarnate.

* * * * * *

Among those who have made the crossing, some have recorded the unequalled bliss of victory. But they have recorded also, according to their different traditions and temperaments, an ensuing and likewise unequalled desolation.

Crowley writes of those who are enduring this latter state, that they "sit as heaps of dust in the City of the Pyramids". St. John of the Cross has much of this experience in his book on the "Dark Night" *(Noche Oscura).* "Since not only the understanding is deprived of its light", he writes, "and the will of its attachments, but likewise the memory is deprived of its cogitation and its contents, the soul might as well have ceased to exist as regards those faculties." (Bk II, Ch. 8,2)

However, this desolation passes, at first intermittently, then lastingly; the presence of the Divine Friend is again known. And known with ecstasy as the Star of the adept's very being.

Not to attempt too close an analysis of those stages of the adept's progress which, so far as can be known on earth, are ultimate, let it be said that as Supernal Binah is at once the sphere of the Supernal Mother, the Neshamah of the individual, and in terms of Jungian psychology the archetypal Anima, so Chokmah is the sphere of the Supernal Father, the Chiah of the individual, and in psychological terms the archetypal Animus. So also Kether is the sphere to which corresponds the Yechidah which is the true unity of the individual, the "Star" as we have called it, the Divine Spark which is the high source and at the same time the inmost radiance of the personality. And whether in earthly life or beyond it, our progress — the progress of any person — can only be fulfilled in reality when the experience of each of these spheres is in due time assimilated.

CHAPTER 12
HEAVENS, HELLS AND THE SOUL

Complex structures

In the World of Briah are the high and glorious beings known as the archangels. There are also the Gods of various pantheons, whose continuing power through the ages is truly to be ascribed to their correspondence to the sephirothic archetypes. In the World of Yetzirah there are the sephirothic choras of angels, with the individual angels of planet, zodiacal sign and element; besides the planetary spirits, innumerable elementals, astral travellers who have temporarily left their earthly bodies, and other entities, some not easily to be classified. There are also the Qlippoth.

Such a description gives the impression of a kind of chaos in the World of Yetzirah, and perhaps also to a lesser degree in Briah. But almost anyone who enters those Worlds by means of the psychic or spiritual faculties has an assurance of meeting with some particular type of the denizens, to the exclusion of others. That is true to some extent, even for those seers who do not guide their perceptive voyaging by conscious intention.

It is, necessarily, a complex structure. For this distinction between the Sephiroth, between the levels of existence, between one pantheon and another or between one mode of thought and another, is founded partly upon objective cosmic order but must also be founded partly upon the personal will, or the range of psychic perception, in the individual. It would therefore be impossible to chart out and to name every distinguishable area of such experience.

It is well known for instance that the particular "hell" which is experienced by those who take narcotics is in some ways akin to, but characteristically different from, the "hell" encountered by alcoholics. But apart from the fact that each is a region of the lower astral, a dark place of Yetzirah, no name is assigned to either. Apart from all else, each person has his own inner "heaven", a personal holy and blissful place to which, when once he has found the way, he can retreat — even if it be but for an instant in a busy day — and be refreshed.

Fortunately it is not within the present task to attempt to chart the whole non-material cosmos. The main areas of its organized structure are known and named in the Qabalistic order of things. The insight which this gives into the nature of the cosmic structure itself, and of a person's own relationship to it, is of great value to the magical student. It can also well serve the mystic, the simple seeker for knowledge, the practical philosopher, and the man or woman who is any or all of these things by turns. But it is not a survey of all known spiritual or psychic experience.

The Sephirothic Heavens

Although there is an occasional variation among authorities regarding the sephirothic Heavens, they are generally stated to be seven in number. They are listed in table 5 of the Correspondences, and in the Notes; none the less, something about their general nature is appropriate here.

The Heavens are attributed to the World of Yetzirah, to the most luminous and elevated region of the Astral Light. It is almost unavoidable to describe these matters as it were topographically. The terms of language are primarily designed to deal with facts concerning the material universe, and in the present context any such description is figurative only; thus if one same non-material region is described as "higher" in one passage and "more inward" in another, the difference will be one of context and there will be no contradiction as to the reality which is indicated. Each sephirothic Heaven is a shining region of joy and inspiration: every sublime concept, every high ideal and noble impulse, every manifestation of beauty and wonder which is associated with the Sephirah itself, is here to be found in the exquisite imagery and vital emotive force of the heights of the World of Yetzirah.

The First Heaven is ascribed to Yesod and Malkuth together. It is the first Heaven to be perceived by the dwellers in Assiah, but still it is in essence a part of the World of Yetzirah.

The two Worlds are not at this stage separable. The splendours of the night sky, for example, belong to the World of Assiah, and so does our physical perception of them; but our experience of that perception rises to another level. Countless aspirants, inspired first by this silent marvel, have been lifted beyond the physical contemplation of it to a sublime awareness of the Yetziratic Heaven: finding through this an intimation of the as yet unknown splendours which await them in the further Spheres, and a glimpse also of the potential of their own nature which has proved capable of apprehending this spiritual promise.

Rightly, the aspirant is dazzled by the wonder of his discoveries and by the illumination which pours into his soul. And the piercing force of this first insight is something he needs to lift his inmost self above any despondent inertia which might otherwise hold him back. For should he not yet have found another key to his personal Heaven — or should this at any time through grief, doubt or fear fail him — he should know he has this other remedy against the ills of the soul: to go and gaze again, awaking the pristine wonder in his heart, at the skies of night. The reason why this Heaven is called "the Veil" needs no other explanation.

As the Qabalist advances in understanding and inner reciprocity with the powers of the Sephiroth, new levels of perception are opened to him: consistent with his spiritual progress, he is enabled meditatively to enter successively into the further Heavens of the Sephiroth in Yetzirah.

But he will not be over-hasty in this, for no-one may gain the experience of a Yetziratic Heaven without due preparation. Initially therefore, knowledge and meditation must encourage emotional response, and emotional response must strike a deep and sincerely meaningful chord within the soul. By this means, specific powers and the appropriate psychic strength will be developed, and the Qabalist will thereby be enabled to enter into the next Heaven.

Further, depending upon the evolution of the faculties of the psyche, the Qabalist may well find in his continuing explorations that his insight and aspiration reach out to yet higher levels, passing beyond the astral Heavens, beauteous though they are, to states of bliss in the World of Briah. Here his questing will touch upon the

Palaces, "states of bliss" truly, modes of being rather than phases of experience; for each Palace is of the purest nature, below Atziluth, of its Sephirah. This level of attainment, while no limitation may be set to it, is for each one who gains it a matter known only in the event. Apart from it, however, entry into each specific Heaven, well prepared for by study and meditation, places the psyche in harmonious rapport with the wondrous intelligences which abide therein; and by contemplation of these beings the Qabalist will gain, whether consciously or unawares, a deep and happy wisdom concerning the Sphere in question.

The Hells: their location and nature

In discussing the Heavens and Hells of the Qabalah, or indeed of any religious or magico-religious structure, one point usually needs to be borne in mind.

Each Heaven or Hell is conceived of as the abode of various spiritual beings, good or bad; it represents in fact that "region" of the non-material universe to which one should direct one's consciousness if one desires to meet with the beings in question. But likewise these beings, good or bad, may be encountered anywhere in what may be termed "neutral territory". This does not separate them from their particular Heaven or Hell. *Their Heaven or Hell is with them where they are.*

The same is true of the human psyche, of incarnate persons as well as of the discarnate. A man or woman may be sitting in the same room with you, conversing with you — yet spiritually he or she may be abiding, removed, in some Heaven or Hell which you may divine if you are sufficiently sensitive, but of which no other person present will ordinarily have any awareness. Every level of the Astral Light, every level, that is, of the World of Yetzirah, can have contact with us in the World of Assiah, just as Yetzirah and each of the other Worlds exist within ourselves.

But when we think objectively of the seven Hells, where do we localise them? They belong to the darkest reaches of the World of Yetzirah, that is, furthest from the influence of Briah and the light of reason. That being so, it will be evident that the Hells cannot be remote from the instinctual levels of our own psychosomatic organisation. However, apart from the ability of the human psyche to create its own private and individual Hell, the question of the states after death must be surveyed on a broad basis, of which, certainly, one aspect is a consideration of the possibility of some human souls remaining after death in any Hell, no matter whether one of the seven or the general and undifferentiated "Hell" of religion.

In looking to the states after death, we may also ask concerning the sephirothic Heavens. Blissful and luminous as is the experience of them, are those Yetziratic abodes to be conceived of as a lasting home for certain souls after physical death? Before tracing the general Qabalistic teachings on the normal course of human destiny, and of some of its main variations within the scope of our theme, it is useful to recapitulate as to the previous development of the psyche according to general Qabalistic tradition.

Involution and Evolution

The seed, or nucleus, of the individual person originates and abides in the Divine Mind, the Mind of the Most High. Being a part of that Mind, it is immortal, incorruptible and forever happy. With the sending forth (so to put it) from the nucleus of a "shining tendril" of itself, the individual Neshamah is formed.

From that occurrence proceeds the involution through the Worlds of the various psychic levels of a specific incarnation, the Ruach and the Nephesh of the personality, towards and into materiality. The evolution from this descent into materiality can then begin.

When a child has been born, its first work is to develop and coordinate the physical body with the Nephesh. Certainly a young child may have intimations of spiritual matters, but these come by way of a direct link which exists between Neshamah and Nephesh. They do not come through the Ruach, which is present but has not yet become developed as part of the personality. Some people continue to have access to this Neshamah-Nephesh link throughout life; it gives rise to what is popularly known as "intuition", but is altogether distinct from the true Intuitive Mind which is the illumination of the Ruach.

At around seven years or sometimes earlier, the development of the Ruach as rational faculty becomes increasingly evident. To master and to direct the faculties which are now accessible is generally the main scope of development of the personality until maturity; but the dawning development of the true Intuitive Mind can reveal itself at any time, before maturity or later.

The great value of an exoteric religion, or of a firm philosophic grounding in the bases of right living, lies in giving a dependable external source of strength and scale of values, until the inner source of true strength and enlightenment is discovered. The balance which it is necessary to maintain in life is this: not the denial to the emotional and instinctual nature, the Nephesh, of its proper development and expression, but the direction and control of it by the Ruach. For the Ruach to allow the irrational faculties, like spoilt children, to dominate the whole personality would be to incur a greater penalty than would at once seem appropriate. A parent might neglect to bring up the children properly, but would suffer acutely if they came to grief as a result.

It is in this regard that the Ruach itself requires to be strengthened and supplemented in its powers of judgment and decision, and in its conviction of the necessity of holding to the ultimate good as this is perceived. Rationality is not enough; not only because the emotions can condition the evidence upon which reasoning is based, but also because the Ruach itself rightly perceives that "cold logic" has too limited a scope to be the supreme arbiter in life. That is indeed a true perception; but the factor which is adequate to supplement the powers of reason is neither biased emotion nor irrational speculation. To realize this purpose worthily, nothing will suffice but that perception of reality which is the gift of the Intuitive Mind. Such a gift in its abundance is not easily nor speedily obtained, but even in its first dawning it begins to complete and fulfil the personality.

The vital decision

There is general agreement among many schools of thought, and the Qabalah upholds it, that with regard to a person's destiny after the close of this life, the important question is the dominant direction of the conscious personality at the time of transition.

At the moment of disseverance from the physical body, the Ruach will be encompassed by a splendour which is the light of the Neshamah. The Ruach, if all is well with it, will spontaneously turn to and accept this splendour, the enfolding glory of its higher, its true self, which will infuse it with new illumination, empowerment and vitality. The Nephesh, taught and matured by a rich emotional life, and habituated to the guidance of the Ruach, will in its measure receive of this light and vitality from the Ruach, with which it will thus be more closely united, to the spiritual gain of both. As for the merely instinctual nature, the "gross astral" or "etheric" body which is a lower function of the Nephesh, this will be relinquished and should not long survive the earthly body, the Guph.

The magical Qabalah envisages this ideal going forth from death, not as a transition into a single glorious but changeless Heaven, but as a progress into sphere beyond sphere of limitless splendours, wonders ever new, in the presence of which the psyche shall grow in understanding, shall go forward in knowledge, shall expand in spiritual capacity and awareness; and if in future place and circumstance it enters again into incarnation, it shall do so refreshed, strengthened, enlightened beyond its former imaginings.

Short of the ideal

If however at the death of the earthly body the entire personality is not rightly orientated, the ensuing sequence of events will be altered, at least for some period of time. Regarding the effects of this alteration, the possibilities are various and opinions concerning them vary even more widely. There are far too many such opinions to be reviewed here, and we shall indicate only the main trend of those which enter significantly into Qabalistic teachings.

The essential spirit, the Neshamah, can in no case be sullied or impaired: it cannot suffer grief, guilt or pain. It is and remains divine. That is not in question. The question is, what can happen to the Ruach, which constitutes the conscious centre of the personality, and what can happen to the Nephesh, of which the fate in every account depends upon the Ruach.

The destruction or irremediable ruin of the Ruach, the operative centre of the consciousness in the personality, is admittedly held in Qabalistic theory to be a possibility, although on psychological grounds it should be a remote one. The Nephesh however, on scriptural and general Qabalistic authority, can certainly be lost.

There may be a situation in which the Ruach, having looked only feebly above mundane concerns during the lifetime and having left the Nephesh to go its own way without cultivation, at the vital moment of decision turns hesitantly and with bewilderment towards the light of the Neshamah. The Ruach itself, lacking the greater understanding which it needs, has not been able in the lifetime to communicate any part of it to the Nephesh. The Nephesh, apathetic and empty, may thus at the death of the body fail of life and disintegrate into the general astral current. The Ruach returning, probably soon, into incarnation, will thus have a new Nephesh with no store of garnered emotional depths.

There is also envisaged a situation in which the orientation of the Ruach is sincerely towards the Higher Self, so that at the moment of decision it clings without hesitation to the light of the Neshamah. Even such a one can however have failed in cultivation of the Nephesh, through a career of dry intellectualism or through a false spirituality which despises the "earthlier" areas of life and fails to see the whole as a divinely-infused unity. The Nephesh, regarded only as a hindrance, can in such a case be reduced to inertia even before physical death.

The loss of the Nephesh must in fact be seen as a possibility in a variety of cases, although frequently, before physical death precipitates such an occurrence, the instincts themselves will find some way to restore in a measure the balance of the personality.

A sidelight

While there are serious warnings, within the Qabalistic structure, as to the need for prudence in one's attitude to life, there is clearly ground for optimism rather than the reverse regarding one's ultimate spiritual destiny. However, speaking realistically in terms of temporal experience, whether in incarnation or beyond, the underworld of the lower regions of Yetzirah should not be belittled. It can be seen in earthly life how the pain of those regions, endured primarily by the Nephesh, can while it lasts seriously impair the action of the Ruach by filling its channels of information with signals of distress.

To win for instance a neurotic away from the self-torturing circlings of the contemplation of a past error is no easy task, as the friend or therapist who undertakes it can recognise; and, too, experience on earth also shows clearly that the duration of a period of intense anguish, whether physical or emotional, cannot be measured according to objective time. Regarding the states after death, there is no reason to suppose that any function of the psyche, freed from the body, is less sensitive than when shielded by it.

Qabalistic variations

Within the scope of such Qabalistic teachings as are generally encountered, there is a sufficient range of views as to the fate of souls whose shortcomings obstruct their progress after death. Briefly, these can be distinguished in two categories: the "punitive state" category and that of the "state of oblivion". It would seem at a first consideration that the latter must the more certainly be an inexorable doom, but this is not necessarily the case: for according to the Zoharic commentary on Exodus, a soul that has once nurtured a right impulse can be "buffeted and awakened" and be brought forth by that right impulse itself, even from Sheol, the deepest Hell of total effacement.

There is also the question as to what functions of the psyche may be involved. Many texts make no distinction in this matter, as if the entire personality were without question involved. Others take into account the different functions of the psyche as these are, for example, distinguished in many passages of the Zohar.

Experience in the depths

Distinctions are rightly made for purposes of study, of magical practice or of therapy, between the different functions of the psyche according to one or another system of classification: yet there is a sense in which, as it is said, "the soul has no parts": each and every function of the psyche *is* the psyche, and represents the whole personality. The evidence of psychic experience likewise indicates the great difficulty of determining what functions of the psyche, exactly, are involved.

Those strong ones who have gone in their own power, or who have been led, to lift an unhappy soul from the lower regions of horror, know how difficult it is: in the first place to secure the attention of such a one, then to awaken first the courage to hope, next a perception of the illiberality and spiritual wastefulness of self-punishment, and finally the operative will to come forth. Necessarily the will in the matter is largely reinforced by that of the helper, but, this aside, there is a general impression that the psychic entity addressed is, or represents, the entire personality. Nor could it seem otherwise. If we take both Ruach and Nephesh to be active there, the Ruach, operating through its vehicle and instrument the Nephesh, will quite naturally not be perceived; while if the Nephesh alone is active, it will be able to communicate effectively, and the non-manifestation of the Ruach is in this case too not likely to be noted. For the presentment of any function of the psyche is a manifestation of that psyche, and will carry the imprint of the same identity. Furthermore, as soon as release from this unhappy bondage is secured, if the functions of the psyche have been separated they will be at once reunited, so that no retrospective view of the question is possible. The one certain conclusion to be drawn from such reports is that Ruach and Nephesh, although in certain circumstances separable, are generally so united that an observer does not easily doubt the active presence of both.

This accords with the general Qabalistic viewpoint. Ruach and Nephesh are indicated by some sections of the Zohar to be essentially one entity: and such they normally are. Each has its own functions, but their interaction is needed at every level for the rich and meaningful experience of life. Death, if not supposed as a complete annihilation — and every kind of evidence is against that (literally) unthinkable supposition — can only be considered as a phase of life. And it is of life, whether incarnate or discarnate, that we tell here. It is of life too that the magical Qabalah teaches.

Life unfolding

We look again at the options after death, when the physical body is lacking but, in compensation, the discarnate soul has greater freedom to find the fulfilment of its true needs.

When we consider the great range of potentialities in the entire field of life, and the equally great adaptability of human nature, we can be confident that whatever have been the experiences of the psyche during an incarnation, yet in its subsequent progress no condition will obtain, in whatever measure of happiness or of suffering, which is not conducive to its ongoing development and wellbeing. What is to be its next stage of progress will be decided, so far as the deepest studies can tell us, by the psyche itself in its great discarnate entirety. For the psyche has its own unmeasured inner life and activity, with an immense vitality and with a scenario and purpose of which modern psychology is still only partially aware.

It would seem to be true of most people that they are habitually of good will and right inclination, in both their Ruach and Nephesh, but yet at the time of transition will stand in need of further enlightenment and greater inner strength.

For these many souls, there is boundless opportunity, as is indicated by the wide compass of the teachings of the Qabalah, and as may be inferred also from the different varieties of formal creed, as well as from living experience both psychic and spiritual. A period of refreshment in the sephirothic heavens or in blissful summerlands may ensue, or the adventure of new experience in the non-material Worlds, developing faculties not given expression on earth; or the consciousness may be expanded by new cosmic perceptions. Or, instead or subsequently, there may be rebirth into the great school of earthly life. By these and by countless other ways, all can be envisioned as able to attain, swiftly or by more gradual steps, to the radiant ecstasy, beyond any description, of their divine realisation.

We aspire now to union with our Higher Self, and so indeed we aspire rightly: but we should not suppose we comprehend the endlessly ongoing glories implied in that union, any more than the astronomers of Ptolemaic times are likely to have guessed what, within even our present knowledge, lay beyond the limits of the physical universe as they charted it.

CHAPTER 13
SONS OF
THE MOST HIGH

The forgotten

Of the uncounted deities to whom sections of the human race have in their time offered adoration, petition and placation, many are known to us by little more than their names. Some are remembered by their names only, or by an unnamed image; doubtless another considerable number are not known even by that much.

Useful speculation has its limits. None the less it can be very relevant for the student of religions — and particularly to the student of magico-religious practice — to enquire what becomes of deities which cease, for whatever reason, to be worshipped.

Why worship ceases

If worshippers in process of time outgrow a primitive concept of deity, they may without making any abrupt change develop a more evolved concept and a more sophisticated system of worship. Alternatively, they may depart from the old system altogether and look elsewhere for one that is more advanced.

Worship of a particular deity may cease because the adherents discover that the effort is all theirs, that no benefit either material or spiritual accrues to them from it. A cult of greater vitality, practised by a neighbouring group, may hasten the desertion of worshippers. Or a cult which was of old time perceived as vital and edifying may have lost its good repute: either because civilisation has left it behind, or because an increasing laxity of practice, of conduct or of belief has warped the cult gradually away from its original intention. New and debased rites may, in any of these cases, be introduced in an attempt to revitalise the cult.

Malefic gods

We have seen how the career of a god begins. Certain human beings, having the requisite mentality and imagination, bring into being an astral likeness of such a deity as they desire. They may already believe in a multitude of spirits, but still a more exact imagining, with a greater intensity of thought, emotion and prayer, will naturally go to the formulation of their deity: whether this be a deity of war, of healing, of the sea, of agriculture or of the family. If their imagining be merely fanciful or in any significant way amiss, the cult is not likely to survive for long; if however the current, so to call it, of an archetype is contacted by their aspirations, a Briatic link is formed and the cult with its new inflow of divine energy will flourish. Prosperity and even, in due course, a perceived code of mystical progress will attend it.

After so fortunate a beginning, and a long continuance, it can none the less happen that a cult will go amiss. A strong but unbalanced personality may become its leading influence. Or trouble may be caused, not by one personality but by many. Of the Briatic being — which is truly "the god", composed of divine and of human energies — the human constituent may gradually become tainted: with greed, with sensuality, with cruelty, or with an appetite for crude Yetziratic manifestations.

If the cult is a strong one the worship may persist, the worshippers continuing to be rewarded — perhaps now with success in crime, perhaps with manifestations of psychic force at festivals of vice and cruelty. Sacrifice whether animal or human is a frequent feature of such cults, the energies of the victims being utilised to disguise the waning of true spiritual power now that the established deity is no longer in accord with the divine archetype.

Such a state of affairs would seem to have been not uncommon, for example, in the Near East in ancient times.

Meaning of Psalm 82

Psalm 82 has suffered from much interpretation by translators of various persuasions, who have striven to express what they severally believed to have been the intention of the psalmist Asaph. The purpose of this present chapter will be better served by an examination of what Asaph has in fact said in this psalm.

Certainly he has employed imagery. Any poet expressing spiritual truth in lyrical form must cast that truth in the likeness, or at least in the vocabulary, of some known human experience. But this is done in a way which does not conceal or vitiate the essential meaning of the utterance.

The first verse of the psalm tells us,

Elohim stands in the assembly of Elohim.

At first sight this statement is enigmatic at several levels. The title Elohim is a grammatical paradox. In its structure it is both feminine and masculine: in syntax it is both singular and plural, and even when plural in meaning it sometimes governs a verb of singular number This divine title must always therefore be considered in exact relation to its context.

As the first word of the psalm, Elohim can plainly be rendered as "God". By Qabalistic usage, this title belongs primarily to Binah as ruler of the Worlds below Atziluth, and, secondarily to Geburah. Elohim is thus a title associated primarily with the supernal Mother, then with the Column of Severity; and this is in harmony with the tone of the psalm. Here we are contemplating the Most High as overseer of the universe, and also as judge and lawgiver.

The second occurrence of the title Elohim is next to be considered. If we do not at once assume it to be different in meaning from the first, we must take the verse to mean, "God stands in his own assembly". We do not, then, at this point possess any clue as to the composition of the assembly, except that it must be made up of a plurality of subordinate beings which are dependent upon God. We look onward for confirmation, and we find in the sixth verse,

I have said ye are Elohim.

These words are plainly addressed by God to the plurality of beings: beings which the psalmist not only in his own person has designated as Elohim, but whom he here designates the Most High as describing as such.

The title Elohim has several accepted meanings. It can refer, as aforesaid, to certain powers and aspects of the Most High. Also, in a general sense, and in Zoharic thought, every Atziluthic potency of the Tree of Life, every Sephirah in the archetypal World, is an Elohim. But in the Hebrew scriptures it is frequently employed, also, to refer to "gods": "the gods of the nations". Passages employing this usage are too numerous to cite, but Exodus 15:11,

Psalm 96:5 and Ezra 1:7 are notable examples.*

Certainly the Elohim intended and addressed in the present context are not human beings, although some translators have tried thus to interpret the matter. Apart from the accepted usages of the title, the fact is brought out clearly by the seventh verse of the psalm:
*Even so, ye shall die like men,
and fall like one of the princes.*

One does not threaten human beings with, "Ye shall die like men". One might say perhaps, "like beasts", or even "like slaves". But "Ye shall die like men", uttered in any age or any region to human beings, must be taken as honorific. These Elohim, moreover, are even threatened with the prospect of falling like a prince.

Quite plainly, however, these words of the psalm are not meant to be honorific. The beings who are addressed are, then, not human beings but are in some manner higher than men, even than men of authority. They are called "Elohim" simply, without a definite article. Unidentified and unnumbered, they can certainly be presumed to be "the gods of the nations".

The doom pronounced by Asaph

We may consider why Asaph chose so enigmatic an opening for this psalm: "Elohim stands in the assembly of Elohim".

The work of one poet influences the thinking of another. Asaph may well have had in mind such a passage as that in the song of David (2 Samuel 22:26,27): "With the merciful thou dost reveal thyself as merciful, with the just thou dost reveal thyself as just ... and with the deceitful thou dost reveal thyself as subtle". So Asaph may have reflected, "With Elohim, gods of the nations, the Most High reveals himself as Elohim, God of Judgment".

Seen in this light, the gods are here bidden to be true to their high function. They are indeed *Sons of the Most High* (verse 6), for they are beings of the World of Briah: gods of like status, although not of the same nature, with archangels, given life and power by a beam of the divine nature from their Atziluthic archetypes. But if they persistently betray their endowment of power, for instance

---

* The title Elohim as applied to the angelic chora of Netzach can here be dismissed as irrelevant.

employing it to favour the unjust, to help in ill deeds those who can afford rich offerings or who promise a share of the plunder, then "the foundations of the earth", that is the maintenance of right conduct and good order at the Yetziratic level, "are shaken": these gods are destroying the faith of many who walk in darkness, and thus they will bring about their own downfall.

"Ye shall die like men"

The death of a god closely parallels the death of a human being. One of the possible causes of death in the case of a god is, in fact, a gross deviation at the Briatic level from the archetype, a deviation which breaks the link which conveyed divine life and power to the humanly formulated structure. In an extreme case such as is here envisaged, the archetypal current, which can in no event have become tainted with evil, withdraws completely to Atziluth, much as the spirit of a human being returns to its source if the psychic structure of that person proves wholly unworthy.

Neither as regards gods nor as regards humankind, however, need these extreme possibilities be taken as a general rule. The Briatic level, true mind, is by its nature attracted to the Atziluthic archetype and this spiritual attraction is not easily to be broken. In the event of corruption at the Yetziratic level — by far the most likely area of disruption — the Briatic level of an established deity (even as the Briatic level of the human psyche) can be supposed most likely to slough off the unworthy lower levels and remain withdrawn to its own World of Briah, there holding to the Atziluthic current which sustains it.

When the flow of power between the higher levels of existence of a god and its Yetziratic formulation has been thus terminated, it can be expected that in the normal course of events earthly worship will die down and cease, like a flame deprived of air. The people will seek other gods, other sources of psychic energy. In process of time, although as regards a once strong cult this may take centuries, the image in the astral, built and animated by the thoughts and aspirations of the worshippers, will dissolve into the astral light, just as a physical corpse crumbles into the undifferentiated dust of earth.

The structure of the godform in Yetzirah does not lose vitality all at once: rather as in the normal course of physical death, the cessation of function of heart and brain, for instance, may not be simultaneous, and the gross astral may persist apart from the body for some days after death has been established. In considering the death of non-corporeal beings, the entire time-scale involved is much greater

Evil gods are not the only deities which die. When the earthly worship of a worthy deity ceases, as may happen from various causes, the Yetziratic image, no longer having that worship to sustain it and perhaps even becoming distorted by hostile emotions, does not now provide an adequate channel for the archetypal and Briatic current. In these circumstances, too, the intellectual form of the god remains at the Briatic level, still vitalised by the Atziluthic current, but without means of conferring benefits or communications to people on earth. Any vestige which remains at the Yetziratic level is likely to dissolve completely as a result of disuse. Further, if in the course of ages worship is not resumed, even the Briatic form of the deity is likely to dissolve also; but when a person of any degree of kindred mentality with the former worshippers truly desires to establish contact, even a vast lapse of time can be a secondary consideration.

The egregores

A Yetziratic god-form is sometimes called an *egregore;* an important term, for it does not signify simply an image. The word is of Greek origin. It comes from a root verb which signifies "to be aware" or "to watch". An egregore is therefore not to be conceived of as a sort of Yetziratic statue, or a doll moulded of astral substance. In fact, the derivation of the word indicates for what use — apart from the creation of god-forms — egregores have from ancient times been shaped by magical practitioners.

The egregore of a god may be brought into being by the worshippers, either spontaneously and unconsciously or as a deliberate creation. Even if the divine current has been withdrawn at either archetypal or Briatic level, the cult of a deity may long persist if the worshippers have discovered, with or without magical understanding, some of the many techniques for releasing and circulating energy at low level among themselves. This, in the nature of things, is the more likely to occur with regard to a cult previously debased; but such is not always the case, and a degraded form of worship may sometimes be found which perpetuates the name and image of a deity once accorded most noble devotion.

In such a cult, some of the energy raised in ceremonial, dance or frenzied prayer will be absorbed by the egregore of the god for its own sustenance, but this need not be noticed by the generality of the worshippers. Physically weak devotees are likely to gain strength in the general circulation of energy, and these will in all sincerity give thanks for their increased vigour. The strong will be disproportionately depleted, but are likely to account their fatigue a small price for the euphoric exaltation of the rites.

Of course an egregore need neither be, nor become, depraved. A right-minded religious group, if it has any vitality, will develop its own egregore even if unknowingly. A magical practitioner may of set purpose create an egregore, which need not be a god-form, for good cause: to watch over a child, to sustain hope in a person depressed, to waken the practitioner from sleep in a specified circumstance, or in fact to perform astrally any one of many good tasks which would be within its power.

Decide by conquest

Throughout history, forms of worship which have been dispossessed by conquest have usually been tragically destroyed or at least severely disrupted at the earthly and Yetziratic levels, no matter what the fidelity of its deities to the archetypes. There are exceptions, as when "captive Greece led captive her captor Rome"; but in that instance the force of a whole civilisation was with the nominally vanquished culture. In many cases the defeated nation, overcome by military or social pressure, falls away from its former worship; the Yetziratic structure generally becoming inadequate to form a channel for the archetypal currents. The egregores in Yetzirah may sink back and disintegrate into the general flow of the astral light, but events show that this is not invariably the case.

In some cultures, certain egregores have been too vital a part of the lives of the people to be easily allowed to perish. A true and hidden worship may for a long time persist, feeding with devotion the attenuated Yetziratic structure, but with the passing of generations this is likely to change.

Practices of folklore, also cherished as part of the old way of life, will be incorporated into the structure. Emotions of grief, resentment and envy, born of oppression, may easily warp the spirit of the worshippers. Moreover the conquerors are likely — a not uncommon step — to denounce the dispossessed deities as demonic. This will not only increase social prejudice and pressure against the cult, but may point it out as a hunting ground to sorcerers who work at the lower astral level, seeking for entities which they can enslave for evil purposes. Such operators cannot, of course, possess themselves of a true Briatic deity, but to take over even an egregore is a prize of considerable worth to them, charged as it will be with the devotional energies of the conquered worshippers.

Wisdom of the priests of Mithras

These eventualities have been fulfilled recurrently with endless variations in the long history of religions. In reflecting upon them, not only the dignity but also the wisdom and the true humanity can be perceived of the final actions of the priesthood of the mysteries of Mithras at Rome, as recounted by Franz Cumont. The mighty and widespread cult of Mithras, which combined in its seven grades the teaching of practical virtue with the mystical doctrine of the Solar Bull, was in the early centuries of Christianity seen as the most powerful adversary of the new religion. It has been said that many of the appurtenances and even the architectural designs adopted by the early Christians were borrowed largely from the practices of the Mithraeum.

Nevertheless the appeal of Christianity, wider and more simple than that of Mithraism, was bound in no long time to give the new faith the ascendancy. The priests of Mithras at Rome, when they saw the defeat of their cult approaching, did not attempt to prolong the struggle. With due rite and form they concluded their worship, obliterated all trace of their ceremonies, closed their temples and vanished into obscurity.

Bridges between World and World

There are considerations in the foregoing which are of importance to students who are drawn to one or another of the ancient pantheons, even if their first intention is only to establish a link of kinship with a bygone culture or way of thought.

The cult of many deities of antiquity is, so to put it, within historical reach, for in many instances the archetypal current has been withdrawn only to the Briatic, not to the Atziluthic level. A person who is sufficiently strongly drawn to one of those deities to make the necessary research, to base upon it a reconstructed or new formula of devotion and thenceforward to persist in it faithfully, can hope to strengthen — or even where need be to renew — the archetypal current.

To establish contact with a deity anciently known and revered, to construct anew the shining bridges between World and World so that the divine archetypal force may flow again in the form and character which it made its own aforetime — this is a worthy work, an inspiring enterprise for the Qabalist. And the rewards are great. A true source of divine power will be there present for invocation, a source carrying the more vigour in the joy of its renewal: and, for him who has re-established it, there will be a focus of beauty and wisdom which has been forgotten by many but which to him will be truly living and potent.

Part 3
THE PATHS
AND THE WAY OF RETURN

CHAPTER 14
THE ASCENT OF THE TREE

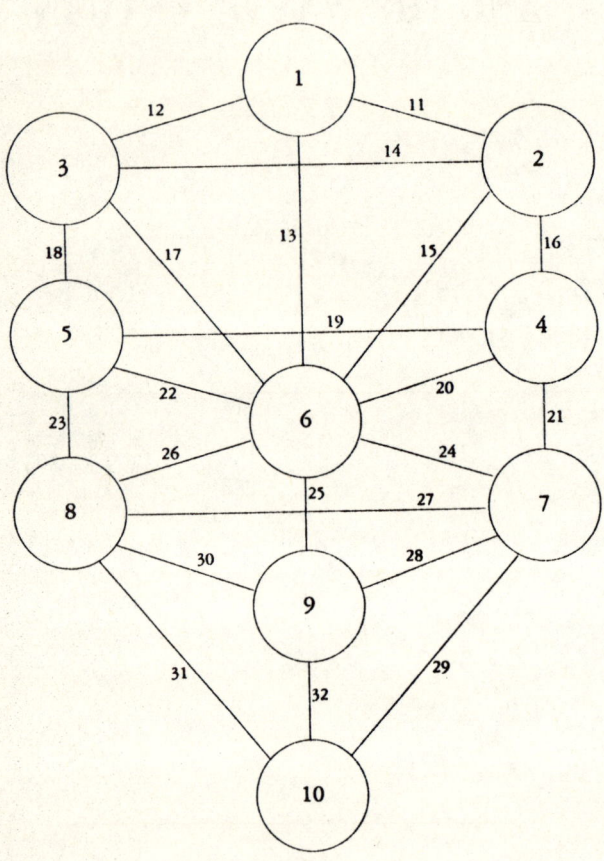

Purpose of the Paths

The full representation of the Tree of Life of the Qabalah shows not only the ten Sephiroth but, crossing and re-crossing in a symmetrical structure, the twenty-two Paths which connect them. Each of these Paths is designated by a letter of the Hebrew alphabet and by the particular influence — planetary, zodiacal or elemental — which is associated with that letter.

Mystically or magically understood, the twenty-two Paths represent a means of transferring the consciousness from the mode of being of one Sephirah to that of another. In their deepest aspect they form a secure means of ascent, guarded by the sacred influences, for the traveller in his inner progress on the Way of Return.

Because these Paths are in their very nature a matter for human experience they are sometimes described as "subjective", while the Sephiroth, being cosmic as well as microcosmic, are "objective". It is also to be understood that in its ultimate application the plan of the Paths is related to the Composite Tree, so that as we proceed from Sephirah to Sephirah we are also able inwardly at certain defined points to proceed from World to World.

The Numbering of the Paths

The Tree of Life is often described as being made up of thirty-two Paths, and from the Tables of Correspondences in Part 4 it can be seen that of these the first ten "Paths" are the Sephiroth.

As "Paths", the Sephiroth can be perceived as in their places on the microcosmic Tree, each included in the grand sequence of the aspirant's ascent. Or they can be understood to form a separate and self-contained system of inner progress, as indeed they do, both by spiritual primacy and by historical record. Nevertheless, when in this book we refer simply to the Paths, it can be understood that the twenty-two Paths specifically are meant, the alphabetic Paths which are numbered from 11 to 32.

The system of spiritual ascent by means of the ten Sephiroth alone, drawn probably from Neo-Platonist concepts, is exemplified particularly by some of the earlier Qabalistic writers, notably Johann Reuchlin and Pico della Mirandola. It is also clearly the basis, although without allusion to the Sephiroth as such, of the spiritual progress of ten ascents described in the *Llama de Amor Viva* ("Living Flame of Love") of St. John of the Cross.

However, the Zohar has its references to the "thirty-two lights," and an authoritative work presenting the full Tree is "The Thirty-two Paths of Wisdom" by the seventeenth-century Qabalist Johannes Stephanus Rittangelius. This deep and subtle work has attracted much criticism on the score of obscurity; but Rittangelius makes considerable use of gematria, the interpretation and correlation of Hebrew words according to the numerical values of their letters, and when this key is applied his pronouncements throw much light upon the nature of each Sephirah and Path with their affinities.

The Letters and the Influences

In turning to the alphabetic Paths we contemplate a matter which, as we come to know it more deeply, is the more truly awe-inspiring. These twenty-two Paths are set in symmetrical order, designated with the letters from Aleph on the 11th Path to Tau on the 32nd, and with their traditionally associated influences: these comprising the seven planets, the twelve zodiacal signs, and the three elements other than earth. The ancient pictographic significance of each letter is also in the background and in many cases fortifies, or even illuminates, the other influence.

These influences could be expected to be most often irrelevant, both to the characters of the adjacent Sephiroth and also to the relationship of a specific Path with other Paths. In fact however — and this is the enduring marvel — each of these influences is not only relevant in both those respects, but is mystically and psychologically right and potent.

Manifold potential

At all stages in the development of the Qabalist there are insights to be gained from reflection upon the Paths and their mystical pageant of Correspondences; for as experience grows, different and more recondite aspects of them will be perceived in luminous aspect. Nor is this true only of the waking life of the Qabalist. As he becomes imbued with these studies (and sometimes even at the very outset of his work with them), occasionally a dream will come which vividly and unmistakably relates to one or other of the Paths. It may introduce quite other symbolism than that to which he is accustomed. To understand such a dream completely and at once is not expected of the dreamer; but it should be recorded as fully as possible and kept, for the greater significance which will probably be seen in it at a future time.

These things being so, it is manifestly impossible to give anything like a complete analysis of the potential of the alphabetic Paths. The main structures must however be given, and systematically; for no matter what sequence the Qabalist may choose for his consideration of the Paths at a later stage, or in what order they may relate to the sequence of events in his outer-world life, their true and proper sequence and some of the reasons for it should be firmly established in his psyche in his student days.

Exploration of the Paths — in meditation, in ritual or in dream — does not necessarily involve passage from World to World, no matter which of the Paths or Sephiroth are in question. Neither is it generally required, in traversing any of the Paths, to take them in their formal order or to work any greater part of the Tree than accords with the purpose of the Qabalist.

Nevertheless, in this one survey we are describing the primal plan of ascent of the entire Tree by the Paths. It is needful to express within this limited compass as much as possible of the immense potential of the Tree, taking into account at the same time its avail for the true spiritual progress, in inner reality, of the aspirant; and for this reason the possible ascents from World to World by means of the Gate-Sephiroth are indicated, in simple terms, where appropriate.

Order, however, does not imply haste. Even supposing, as we do in this "model" survey, that our traveller is following out strictly the plan of the Way of Return (which, most often, need not and will not be the case) there is no intrinsic ruling as to the time of the journeying and reflection upon the respective Paths. Assuredly the traveller will be eager to pursue his quest of the Paths without undue delay, but assuredly also he will take time to review and to digest — and, desirably, to record also — that which he has experienced. As regards the periods of time involved, no more than that can be said.

Status of the Influences upon the Paths

Elsewhere in this book, situations have been envisaged in which the assimilation and inward resolution of a force has been an advanced, even a perilous work. Upon the Paths however the assimilation of the attributed influence is altogether beneficent, giving strength and enhightened faculties to the psyche. What takes place here is in reality the *reassimilation* of an influence which is a true part of the psyche of the operator. Such an influence may have been given objectivity by the action of the unconscious mind in stress of emotion or in dream, or it may have been deliberately endowed with objectivity for the purpose of identification and dialogue, as in meditation. Every planetary or zodiacal influence, and the influence of every element, is by nature present in the psyche, whether in a dominant or a regressive state. To distinguish and to identify every such influence, and to give it its rightful place and proportion in the whole, is to gain a more extended awareness of one's own potential and command of one's faculties.

For the Tree that the Qabalist is now exploring is the Tree within his own psyche: and in so far as he knows and governs it, he knows and can govern his world.

Attaining the Gate of Yesod

The first step which must be accomplished is that which in fact reverses the last step of the descent into materiality: the Path from Malkuth to Yesod. This is the 32nd Path, to which is ascribed the letter Tau, "the Sign of Identification". The Path carries also the influence of Saturn, a reflection as it were from the cold and sombre light of that planet.

A part of the significance of this Saturnian guardianship may be early seen. Those who attempt to take by storm the Astral Light — the World of Yezirah at large — without first achieving the Gate of Yesod, are liable to find themselves helpless where they thought to be masters, assailed by all the deceits of the illusory aspect of Yetzirah, with its illimitable array of sexual and grandiose fantasies. Saturn is the planet of discipline and of reward for discipline accepted, so that its guardianship upon this Path enables the traveller to hold securely to reality. But the matter is more trenchant even than that.

Beginners upon the Way of Return, after an initial burst of high aspiration and exaltation frequently fall into an opposite extreme of almost intolerable dejection. Either they have a feeling that any attempt at progress would be futile, or they simply feel unable to summon the will to proceed.

Those victims of this state who know something of the language of mysticism will sometimes declare with conviction that they are entering upon the Dark Night. No doubt there is something of the high-flown delusiveness of Yetzirah in this, but there is also a grain of valid cause for the surmise. For the gloom of Saturn is echo and portent of the cosmic night of Binah.

Not every beginner has to endure the experience of this painful dejection, but when it comes the only remedy is to accept it and to persist none the less in one's resolve. There may come doubts and fears of all kinds, but this is not the time to oppose them with reasoning. This is a Path of darkness, of unknowing; but upon it as upon every Path there is an angel who will aid. It is an illusory ordeal, and not a long one. Whether the aspirant encounters its darkness involuntarily in ordinary consciousness, or by a chosen meditative encounter, or in sleeping dream and in subsequent reflection, that darkness has to be accepted as part of the aspirant's self, and inwardly resolved.

The mastery of Yesod once achieved, the psyche enters into awareness of its own great potential at the astral level, and gains that equilibrium in the World of Yetzirah which opens the way to its further progress. Now the traveller is free to explore and to delight in the continual wonders of Yesod. The astral level of Malkuth, too is open to him if he wishes to linger awhile over its secrets. But not only Yesod and Malkuth are open to him now; in the World of Yetzirah there are other Paths to travel and other Sephiroth to visit.

The Paths to Hod

The traveller can now address himself to the 31st Path, that is, the Path from Malkuth to Hod. The chief influences upon this Path are the letter Shin and elemental Fire.

Here is an immediate challenge. Moving from the complex life of Earth towards the cool energy of the Sphere of Mercury, we pass through the keeping of Fire and of the angel of Fire. The letter Shin represents "the Tooth": this fire is a devouring flame.

Whatever the influence upon a particular Path, the experience in traversing it is necessarily affected at the beginning by the ambience of the Sephirah of origin, and at its close by the ambience of the Sephirah of conclusion. Upon this 31st Path, fire is perceived and experienced in all the aspects of its elemental nature, fierce, destroying, yet incorruptible, strong and exulting in its ever-changing, terrible beauty. Yet as the traveller approaches the subtle and luminous mode of being which is the Sephirah Hod, the elemental fire of the Path is no longer perceived as a wild force, but as fire brought within bounds and skilfully controlled in the furnace of the alchemist to the exact degree required for a particular phase of the Great Work.

When the Sephirah has been entered the consideration of the work of the alchemist may well be maintained, for now the fire of the Path, having been tempered and assimilated, will be brought fully into balance by its association with the other three elements, water, air and earth in a true operation of the inner alchemy of the psyche.

The traveller who follows this line of imagery, upon entering into Hod and meditating thereon can find many truths disclosed concerning both the universe and himself, for alchemy has ever explored the outer and inner worlds in synchronicity. And as can be seen with every other Sphere which is gained, the influences on each Path of access give a characteristic perspective upon the Sphere itself.

Hod having been entered from Malkuth, the next exploration is undertaken by the 30th Path, from Yesod. The strong imaginative energy bestowed by the Sephirah of commencement gives added light and power to this Path: gives, indeed, most vital light and power. The chief influence here is that of the letter Resh, "the Head", associated with that of the Sun. While here again we have a fiery influence, this is not simply an elemental force, but a force cosmic and most particularised. The experience of this Path is therefore of a different and more intense character than that of the one preceding. To traverse it is in some degree to make contact with the primal cosmic force which has called forth the life of our world, and has given one of the chief bases of our patterns of action and of thought. This mighty influence can but be encountered in absolute simplicity, but in proceeding upon this Path the traveller is inwardly raised up by a deep gladness and confident hope; and these, besides the counterpart of the solar power itself, he recognises to be of the true nature of his psyche.

If the 31st Path led the traveller, after entering Hod, to explore something of the equilibrating work of alchemy, the 30th will bring him when he has entered that Sephirah to behold in some manner the work of transmutation itself. What he experiences will not be the transmutation of his personality — that is not for this Sphere — but a foretaste of it, for which he will have been conditioned by the solar power in which he has journeyed. Under whatever form it may be evoked, this manifestation — even though perhaps as yet but the Yetziratic manifestation — of Hod as the veritably alchemical and magical Sephirah, will disclose itself in terms of change and renewal.

The Paths to Netzach

The relationship which can be perceived between the first two Paths to Netzach presents an evident parallel to that existing between the Paths to Hod. The cool ambience of Hod is approached by two Paths of a fiery nature; the genial fires of Netzach are approached by two Paths which have an affinity with water.

The 29th Path, from Malkuth, has as its chief influence the letter Qoph, "the Back of the Head". Associated with it is the Sign of Pisces, the Fishes, the most humble Sign in the Zodiac. The traveller may feel impelled to approach the Sphere of Love as if he were masked. It is not a bad guise, to be an anonymous member of the gentle and shimmering throng which symbolises this Path. But self-effacement must be put aside before he enter the Sphere of Netzach, which is Victory.

The 28th Path, which leads from Yesod to Netzach, is a Path of great charm and fascination. That much, certainly, could be anticipated from its Spheres of commencement and of destination. Carrying all the imaginative potency of Yesod at the outset of the journey towards the Sephirah of the mighty forces of life and of love, this Path has as its governing influence an alluring and intoxicating force which is represented by the letter Tzaddi, "the Fish-Hook". The attributed influence is the zodiacal Sign of Aquarius, that mysterious figure who carries the waters of life in his pitcher.

Even the aware and experienced traveller may still take heed, for although the fascination may be recognised, the Path from Yesod to Netzach is always one of great magnetism, and even assimilation is not an all-powerful weapon. From its commencement to its completion it represents a force which, however clearly we recognise it as a part of our own nature, can always objectivise itself and meet us (so to express the matter) with the enigmatic face of a stranger. But the traveller who is fully intent upon his goal enters by this Path into a vision of the reality of Netzach, in which the triumph of love and beauty is celebrated in light and colour, with flashes of brighter illumination which enhance all and yet show most faithfully the true dignity and glory of the Sphere.

Hod and Netzach: a confrontation?

Less immediately plain is the reason for the influence upon the next Path, the 27th, which passes from Hod to Netzach. This Path carries the letter Peh, "the Mouth", with the influence of the planet Mars. Why is the force of Mars encountered here, and why does it need to be assimilated by the traveller before he can pass to Netzach by this road in particular?

The power of Hod is strongly magical but it can also be very coldly scientific, Furthermore, Hod is situated upon the column of Severity as also is Geburah, the Sphere of Mars. Netzach, upon the Column of Mercy, is the Sphere of natural life and love. In the movement and action of what we may term the spirit of Hod towards Netzach, what is the threat of this force of Mars? If such a threat is seen it cannot be lightly dismissed, for in the order of things the forces of nature and those of science or of magic are interdependent, as are also the human practitioners whose specialities they are. How then is this natural reciprocity threatened by an apparently needless intrusion of Mars?

It can be recognised in external life. An obvious example occurs when an application of natural laws is developed for peaceful purposes and is taken over for military use. But more apposite examples have been seen, occurring altogether within the area of medicine

There have been occasions when a drug has been developed with the intention of conferring health and wellbeing upon sufferers from a specific malady, or upon people generally, or perhaps for agricultural use. All such are concerns of Hod directed towards Netzach. But impatience, or rivalry, or a contempt for paperwork, combined in any case by great over-optimism — these faults all being of the nature of Mars in imbalance — have led to the drug being marketed before being adequately tested; and health and happiness, the concerns of Netzach, have been seriously impaired thereby.

It befits the traveller upon the 27th Path to give objective form, in whatever mode seems to him the most suitable, to the force of Mars as he finds it in his own nature, that it may be brought into the control of inner equilibrium before he seeks to enter Netzach by this Path.

The Paths to Tiphareth

Thus far the sequence of ascent of the Paths has followed a simple numerical countdown. Now however a special complexity supervenes.

Three Paths lead to the great Gate-Sephirah of Tiphareth. By only one of them can the aspirant (let us so designate him) whose will it is, initially attain to Briah; but before he can do so he must have experience of all three Paths. This is like a folk-tale, but in view of the nature of these Paths it makes true psychological sense.

The 26th Path leads from Hod, from the Pillar of Severity. The influence upon this Path is that of the letter Ayin, the name of which signifies "the Eye", but by an ancient alternative meaning — it is not even a play on words — it is also Ayn or Ain, "the Well". Both the Eye and the Well are primal guardians of life, but both have their perilous aspect for each is in its own manner insatiable. The power which is to be governed and assimilated upon this Path, so far as each traveller can do so, is indicated by the associated zodiacal Sign, Capricorn. It is that of the desirable quality, the worth and beauty, of material things; and though the mountain goat can reach the highest peaks, he cannot help but stand upon the rock of elemental Earth. The aspirant inwardly follows this Path to the very portal of Tiphareth, but — until he has gained the Sephirah by another route — he proceeds no further.

His next sally is from Netzach, from the Pillar of Mercy. This Path, the 24th, has as its chief influence the letter Nun, "the Fish", with the Sign Scorpio; in astrology this Sign leads the native to explore the spiritual deeps and with stout heart to seek an understanding of the powers of death. This Path has its perils also, for the sensation of death itself and perhaps the darkness of the deeps must be accepted here; but as in his experience of the previous Path, although the aspirant win through to the very gate of Tiphareth, he does not yet find admittance.

The trial of the 24th Path having been balanced against that of the 26th, the aspirant's next approach is made by the 25th Path upon the Column of Equilibrium. He begins his progress from Yesod, which is now for him not a region of illusion but the Foundation of his established mastery in the World of Yetzirah. The letter upon the 25th Path is Samekh, the Support. The attributed influence here is the Sign Sagittarius, of which the Hebrew name is Qashat, the Bow. One can imagine the bow of the crescent moon, in Yesod, from which an arrow of light speeds unerringly towards the Sphere of the Sun. Unerringly too our aspirant speeds upon his inward journey: for it is by this Path that he makes his entry into the glorious Sephirah of Tiphareth and wins his exaltation into the mysteries of Briah.

Having gained Tiphareth, he will begin to develop the Briatic consciousness and perception which is a function of the Intuitive Mind: a power perhaps not at once perceived, not to be enjoyed at once in its fullness, but increasing with time, with use and with reflection.

But the task he should undertake, before proceeding further, is to return to the experience of those Paths by which previously he failed to enter Tiphareth. He returns to Hod, to survey with new vision that Sphere of wonders. Even now he perceives that much which previously seemed to him a subject for intricate reasoning — no strange experience in the lower aspects of this Sephirah — has another aspect, to be grasped by the inner sight as shining and evident truth, exquisite in its clarity. From there he travels again the 26th Path, and looks with the eyes of enlightened Mind upon all the majestic beauty and the shining treasures of nature and of art. He sees them, not as anything to be either coveted or rejected, for the world is a part of his life and his life is a part of it; he gazes upon these things with love and joy, and having come to the Gate of

Tiphareth he enters in.

Now he revisits Netzach, to see in a clearer and more steady light the radiant shapes, the growing and moving patterns of life itself in that Sephirah. To the mind which apprehends them, any contact with these many-hued and luminous beings is a source of delight and of love, but this is not the occasion for him to linger, and he takes again the 24th Path.

Here with the eyes of Mind he beholds distinctly not only physical death as a reality, but also that darker spectre which makes it fearful, that strong instinctive dread of the unknown which the psyche holds in its hidden places. He sees that death is a needful episode in the journey of life, but that this other gulf is stark unreason. He looks directly upon death with neither fear nor contempt, but as the sign of a great mystery without which neither birth nor renewal could come about; and so he arrives at the gate of Tiphareth, and once more enters in.

As his new perception in the Briatic consciousness grows, all the marvels of Yetzirah and of Assiah that he has previously experienced will be enhanced a thousandfold in the light of a spiritual Sun; and in this same progress Tiphareth itself, and in due course the other Sephiroth proper to the World of Briah, will be ever more significantly and vitally disclosed to him, so to open the onward road.

Above Tiphareth

In whatever mode the Qabalist may in practice work the Paths, to traverse them is in itself an adventure in inner space. The whole range of the Correspondences, written and unwritten, can be summoned if desired to enhance his experience and to diversify its outward apparel. Upon these Paths above Tiphareth, it is likely that he who travels them in the World of Yetzirah will require more external assistance than upon the lower Paths, whereas he who experiences these higher Paths in the World of Briah may find little or no need for the use of material devices. But in whatever mode and in whichever World the Paths collectively are traversed, what is experienced is never less than a part of the awakening and training of the entire psyche in preparation for its glorious destiny.

In techniques Western and Eastern, each small part of the physical body is given consideration and is manipulated or exercised in order to awaken it to a fuller consciousness of its proper activity. In fact each of these small parts is by increased circulation and nerve-stimulation brought into more complete coordination with the whole: and it is this coordination and integration, not the isolated experience of each nerve and muscle, which is the true purpose of the procedure. So it is with the psyche, and with our purpose upon the Paths: the whole psyche is enriched and brought into greater unity through the exercise of its various fields of activity, and through the recognition, reintegration and reassimilation of those functions which are designated as the influences upon the Paths.

As the numbering of the Paths indicates, the traveller does not in any event proceed directly from Tiphareth to the higher Sephiroth. The next Path taken is the 23rd, which runs from the potently magical Sephirah of Hod up to Geburah which is Strength itself. The letter upon this Path is Mem, its intrinsic significance reinforced by the attributed influence of elemental Water. The power of the Supernal Mother is reflected here, certainly because the Column of Severity is under her dominance, but also because the underlying idea of her great emblem the primal ocean is evoked. Here is a power more immense than that of any one Sephirah, but more gentle in manifestation. So the traveller comes though an intimation of that mighty potency which is the cradle of all, into the austere Sephirah of Strength.

After the ascent to Geburah from Hod comes the ascent to Geburah from Tiphareth: a passage from the Sun-sphere in the central equilibrium of the Tree to the Sphere of Mars on the Column of Severity. The traveller upon this Path, the 22nd, makes the transition within another ambience of equilibrium, for here, attributed to the letter Lamed, "the Ox-Goad", is the influence of the Sign Libra, the Balance.

Wings upon the Ascent

At this stage in the ascent a strange and inspiring thing occurs, although in the experience the shape of it may not at once become apparent.

Below Tiphareth, shown in a straight line with this 22nd Path is the 24th, which comes from the Sphere of Venus. Now Venus is the ruling planet of Libra; and a zodiacal Sign, although carrying intrinsically no major charge of the influence of its ruling planet, is a most apt vehicle to convey, and thus to intensify where it exists, the power of that planet. Here the power of Netzach-Venus, most potently exalted and glorified by its projection through Tiphareth, is again carried and amplified by the influence of Libra which enwraps the traveller on his way to Geburah.

This supremely heightened empowerment is however but the first part of the marvel, the full significance of which remains to be shown.

From the Column of Severity the action moves across to the Column of Mercy. The 21st Path leads from Netzach to Chesed, and upon it, with the letter Kaph, "the Palm of the Hand", is the influence of Jupiter. After the powerful experience of Geburah, to be thus steeped in the Jupiterian influence is the only preparation adequate for entrance into Chesed, the Sephirah of boundless generosity, of abundance, of all that makes life expansive and joyous.

Chesed having been entered by this Path, the pattern which has been established regarding the 24th and 22nd Paths, is again followed. A new approach to Chesed is made from Tiphareth, by the 20th Path. Below Tiphareth, shown in a straight line with this 20th Path is the 26th, which commences from Hod, the Sphere of Mercury. Mercury is the ruling planet of the zodiacal Sign Virgo, which is the influence on the 20th Path. Thus the power of Hod-Mercury, most potently exalted and glorified by its projection through Tiphareth, is carried and amplified by the influence of Virgo which infuses the traveller upon this Path to Chesed.

These two Paths, the 22nd and the 20th, carrying respectively the transmuted power of Netzach to Geburah and of Hod to Chesed — carrying Victory to Strength and Splendour to Magnificence — give an immense empowerment to those high Sephiroth in the psyche of the traveller of the Paths. Besides this, the Paths themselves form as it were two mighty wings, to raise the journeying of the traveller in Briah particularly to the higher spiritual levels of that World, and to fortify him for the realisation of those levels with singleness of purpose maintained in equilibrium.

The linking of the Columns

The 19th Path, from Geburah to Chesed, sets a seal upon this portion of the work. It unites the Columns of Severity and Mercy, which in their lower phases of action are to be seen in a possible opposition: and it unites them at the most characteristic points of their respective manifestations. The chief influence upon this path is the coiled Serpent of the letter Teth, to which is attributed the zodiacal Sign of the Lion. The inward linking of Geburah to Chesed is thus recognised as a work which calls for great spiritual power.

It is a true Briatic perception not merely to know as a fact, but to apprehend in the beauty of its reality, that Justice and Mercy are but two aspects, fully distinct from one another but without division, of one act of the Divine Mind. Man can exercise justice without mercy, or be merciful to the outrage of justice, but the action of the divine nature is otherwise. Furthermore, not only to see this, but to be able to accept it as a principle in one's attitude to life, requires great fortitude. In the inner space of the psyche the serpent Teth binds the Columns together: the heart of the Lion affirms, "Thus it is and shall be".

The higher progress

Beyond this point the travelling of the Paths is diagrammatically clear, but in practical terms variable. St. John of the Cross indicates his "seventh ascent", which to us is the Sphere of Jupiter or the Sephirah Chesed, as the point from which further attempted spiritual progress is particularly liable to a fall. That is true, because any one of the great qualities associated with this Sephirah can be perilously intoxicating to human nature without giving any indication of danger. Here, before the World of Atziluth can be mystically gained, we have the barrier of the Abyss and the vast steeps which separate even the high Spheres above Tiphareth from the Supernals.

As the diagram of the Tree shows, there is no direct Path from Chesed to Binah. There is no Path even for the traveller who is making his way in meditation, imaginatively through the World of Yetzirah, or mentally through the World of Briah with as yet no intention of venturing beyond.

Certainly it is entirely within the power of the human imagination or intellect at this stage to approach and enter the Sephirah Binah by the 18th and 17th Paths of the Tree; but the entrance gained thereby will be of the lower aspect of the Sephirah, the mode of being represented by the planetary Sphere of Saturn. The supernal plenitude of the third Sephirah cannot be experienced without the Atziluthic consciousness which is the spiritual fruit of crossing the Abyss by the Gate of Daath.

However, leaving aside for the present the question of the Abyss and the transition to a yet higher level, to continue upon the Paths in Briah the first approach to Binah is by the 18th Path from Geburah. The Geburah in the psyche of the meditative traveller who has ventured thus far has been fortified by the indomitable life-force of Netzach through Tiphareth; but even so the keyword upon this Path is prudence. The letter of this Path is Cheth, "the Fence", and the influence attributed thereto is that of the Sign of Cancer. The armour of the Crab is clearly relevant, and so is its habit of sideways movement: this approach from Geburah, when a Path from Chesed might have been looked for, is an indication to the same purpose. At the same time, the ruling planet of Cancer is the Moon, and at these levels the higher power of the Moon is of great significance. Her bright disc can be seen as a shield, and the Moon is most anciently a symbol of the Great Mother herself, Queen of the Universe, another of whose symbols is, again, the Crab. It is her protection, then, that the traveller is to seek in approaching even a lower outwork of her citadel.

Of the entrance to the Sphere of Binah-Saturn and the experience of that great and brooding Creativity, it remains only to recall that this too takes place within the ambience of the traveller's psyche. This does not vitiate its validity, for the psychic counterpart of the Sphere, as that of every Sphere, stands in direct relationship to its cosmic prototype.

The other Path to Binah-Saturn is the 17th, from Tiphareth. The influence upon this Path is that of the zodiacal Sign, Gemini. The letter is Zayin, "the Sword" so that the interpretation of the Twins here would seem to be of one divided rather than of two united. Indeed, the commencement of this Path in Tiphareth seems to bring a transmuting quality to the ensuing experience, a divine lightness and a swift brilliance, over against the Saturnian calm of the destination. But also the ruling planet of Gemini is Mercury, and in mythology Mercury is the divine messenger whose function it is to bring tidings from the world of the gods. The element of both Sign and planet is Air, and where even the footfall of the mind finds no way, the winds of the spirit may carry us.

Whatever the personal intent, at this time, of the traveller upon the Paths who has thus come to the third Sephirah without having gained the Atziluthic consciousness, the message of this Path from Tiphareth is that his spiritual journey should not, indeed will not, rest for unmeasured time at this point. We here contemplate the region where — no matter which the World of our questing — the hold upon earthly habits of thought, even the most elevated, must be in some degree loosened if we are in any manner to apprehend what lies before us.

The Divine Magnetism

For the further course, the entrance into Supernal Light and Life, we turn to contemplate the traveller who in Briatic consciousness has progressed so far as to enter into Chesed from the 19th Path, and whose fixed intent it is to gain the crowning consciousness of the divine World of Atziluth. To win that incomparable prize he will hazard not only all that he has, but all that he is. He will travel the uncharted way from Chesed in the World of Briah through the mysterious Gate of Daath, passing the Abyss to Supernal Binah: not by force of will alone, but because at this moment of his personal evolution his entire being responds to the call, the magnetism, of his Higher Self, his Star in Atziluth.

The entrance into Daath, the passing of the Abyss, and the entrance into Supernal Binah, belong to a time beyond time, a knowledge beyond knowledge. This cannot be contemplated in terms of the imagination, nor of the thinking mind; it cannot be compared to birth or to death because it does not involve the physical body, and yet it must have spiritual kinship to both of these. The intimations of the Intuitive Mind will in the past have brought the voyager — the attained, we may truly call him — into perceptions far above the processes generally reckoned as thought; now he goes beyond those intimations into an instant of direct perception of truth through the medium of Spirit. Even without awareness of time, he can remain but briefly in that experience. Subsequently, and while he remains in incarnation, his Atziluthic consciousness will be as it were veiled, although he is now entirely within the guidance of his Star, his Higher Self.

We can contemplate something of his progress on the Paths of the Tree, for his inner life is still within their compass, but that progress in the World of Atziluth is entirely as his Star shall direct.

If now he travel the 18th and 17th Paths, they too will bring him again into his attained Sphere of the Supernal Mother. But he will also traverse the 16th and 15th — the steadfast resolve of the Path of Vau and the luminous window of the Path of Heh, into the perception, immeasurably sublime, of the Supernal Father, and then make the transition from Binah to Chokmah in the resplendent glory of the 14th Path of Daleth, the Door, whose influence, Celestial Venus, unites all things in peace and power.

From that point it is his to assimilate the experience of the 12th and 11th Paths, in recognition and fulfilment of the two great spiritual polarities of his being. That assimilation completed, there follows in the maturity of time a supreme affirmation of his true will: Thence, in the high radiance and joy of the supernal light, he takes that direct Path which in Yetzirah and Briah is the 13th, but which in Atziluth is the final Path, leading into the ultimate Gate of divine union.

In Yetzirah and Briah the 13th Path may be experienced emotionally and intellectually as the Path of integration perfected, and thus it may be retraced often for further comprehension of its mystery. But its influence is the Moon in her highest aspect and its letter is Gimel, "the Camel", which traverses the silent and desert ways of mystery. In Atziluth this Path is the crowning journey of soul and spirit, and whoso goes by this way does not turn aside to the house of either Mother or Father. Directly and swiftly by this Path the mystic passes on to his goal, and enters into Light Illimitable.

An Overview

Such, in brief compass, is a survey of the Paths of the Tree of Life and of some of the wonders of the Way of Return which they outline for us. An important aspect of the matter has, necessarily, been touched upon at but a few points, and that briefly: it is the interaction of the inner life with the outer, which differs in detail for every person.

Naturally, in the interlace of inward and outward life the sequence of the Paths is, seemingly at least, often disordered. A person who has progressed far in meditation may be suddenly confronted with an earthly occurrence which gives a crude presentation of one of the lower Paths, and which requires his involvement and decision. Or a student who has just begun to take a serious interest in the Way of Return may have a vivid dream which relates to a high mystical level.

There is no real difficulty in these things. Because our conscious mind can give attention only to one subject at a time, we tend to think of ourselves as living on only one level at a time. That is far from the truth. Different areas of the psyche simultaneously live their lives, not only at different levels but frequently at a different tempo from one another.

One of the great integrating therapies of work on the Paths consists in the fact that, moving systematically through the Paths and the Spheres it gives every overt or hidden component of the psyche its opportunity to speak, in meditation or, more freely, in dream. But the outward and seemingly disconnected happenings of life are governed from within more often than is generally guessed. To gain control of such occurrences, for peace of mind and serenity of life, is a motive which can particularly commend regular work and reflection upon the Paths to the Qabalist.

But that is not the greatest matter. The joy of the Paths, of traversing and re-traversing them, resides in the consistent yet ever-changing stream of truth, of wonder, of new comprehension which they present. It is a stream which overflows into the outer life, not distorting it but enriching it with significance, and with gleams even of glory. Yet it is more than an overflowing, it is a manifestation of the unity of the inner and outer life, and the reality becomes more realized and more evident as we progress. For that which we are within affects, inevitably, our relationship to the entire world, to the entire universe.

Seen from this viewpoint, the distinction between inner and outer reality ceases to exist; external activity and meditation are alike parts of the experience of life, and the Paths upon which at every level we prepare ourselves all lead, in their ultimate development, to that divine life which is beyond Time.

Part 4
CORRESPONDENCES

1 — THE TEN SEPHIROTH

Sephirah	Hebrew name	Transliteration	Meaning
1	Kether	KThR	Crown
2	Chokmah	ChKMH	Wisdom
3	Binah	BYNH	Understanding
4	Chesed, Gedulah	ChSD, GDVLH	Mercy, Magnificence
5	Geburah	GBVRH	Strength
6	Tiphareth	ThPARTh	Beauty
7	Netzach	NTzCh	Victory
8	Hod	HVD	Splendour
9	Yesod	YSVD	Foundation
10	Malkuth	MLKVTH	Kingdom

2 — SEPHIROTHIC DIVINE NAMES

Sephirah	Hebrew name	Transliteration	Significance
1	Ehyeh	AHYH	Unqualified divine being
2	Yah	YH	Divine creativity
3	YHVH Elohim,	YHVH ALHYM	The pleroma
4	El	AL	God
5	Elohim Gebor	ALHYM GBVR	Divinity
6	YHVH	YHVH	The Lord in manifestation
7	YHVH Tzabaoth	YHVH TzBAVTh	Manifest Lord of Hosts
8	Elohim Tzabaoth	ALHYM TzBAVTh	God (Divinity) of Hosts
9	El Shaddai	AL ShDY	All-powerful God
10	Adonai	ADNY	Lord

3 — PLANETARY COLOURS AND METALS

Sephirah	Planet	Colour (Spectrum)	Colour (Ptolemaic)	Metals
3	Saturn	Indigo	Grey	LEAD, antimony
4	Jupiter	Blue	White	TIN, pewter, zinc
5	Mars	Red	Fiery red	IRON, the steels
6	Sun	Yellow	Gold	GOLD, yellow alloys
7	Venus	Green	Saffron	COPPER, red alloys
8	Mercury	Orange	Nacre	QUICKSILVER, aluminium alloys
9	Moon	Violet	Silver	SILVER, white metals
10	Earth	Spectrum	—	—

4 — THE HEAVENS OF ASSIAH

Sephirah	Hebrew name	Transliteration	Meaning
1	Rashith ha-Gilgalim	RAShYTh H-GLGLYM	Primal Whirlings
2	Mazloth	MZLVTh	The Destinies (Zodiac)
3	Shabbathai	ShBThAY	The Restful (Saturn)
4	Tzedeq	TzDQ	The Righteous (Jupiter)
5	Madim	MDYM	Garment, or Covered Throne (Mars)
6	Shemesh	ShMSh	The Sun
7	Nogah	NVGH	Brightness (Venus)
8	Kokab	KVKB	The Star (Mercury)
9	Levanah	LBNH	Whiteness, Purity (Moon)
10	Cholem Yesodoth	ChLM YSVDVTh	Strength of the Foundations

5 — THE SEVEN HEAVENS OF YETZIRAH

Sephirah	Hebrew name	Transliteration	Meaning
1,2,3	Araboth	ORBVTh	Plains
4	Makon	MKVN	Established place, City
5	Ma'on	MOVN	Refuge
6	Zebul	ZBVL	Habitation
7	Shechaqim	ShChQYM	Clouds
8	Reqia	RQYO	Expanse, Canopy
9,10	Vilon	VYLVN	Veil (of the Heavens)

6 — THE SEVEN HELLS

Sephirah	Hebrew name	Transliteration	Meaning
1,2,3	Sheol	ShAVL	Effacement
4	Abaddon	ABDVN	Destruction
5	Bar Shachath	BAR ShChTh	Pit of Corruption
6	Tit ha-Yeven	TYT H-YVN	Quagmire
7	Shaare-Maveth	ShORY-MVTh	Gate of Death
8	Tzal-Maveth	TzL-MVTh	Shadow of Death
9,10	Ge-Hinnom	GY-HNM	The Gully of Hinnom

7 — THE SEVEN PALACES IN BRIAH

Sephirah	Hebrew name	Transliteration	Meaning
1,2,3	Hekel Qadosh Qadeshim	HKL QDVSh QDShYM	Palace of the Holy of Holies
4	Hekel Ahabah	HKL AHBH	Palace of Love
5	Hekel Zakuth	HKL ZKVTh	Palace of the Purified

130   Entrance to the Magical Qabalah

6	Hekel Ratzon	HKL RTzVN	Palace of Joy
7	Hekel Etzem Shemaim	HKL OTz ShMYM	Palace of the Essence of the Heavens
8	Hekel Thushiah	HKL ThVShYH	Palace of Abundance, of Wisdom
9,10	Hekel Garen ha-Saphir	HKL GRN H-SPYR	Palace of the Court of Lapis

8 — THE SEPHIROTHIC CHORAS OF ANGELS

Sephirah	Hebrew name	Transliteration	Meaning
1	Chayoth ha-Qadosh	ChYVTh H-QDSh	Holy Living Ones
2	Ophanim	AVPNYM	Wheels
3	Aralim	ARALYM	Strong Ones
4	Chashmalim	ChShMLYM	Shining Ones
5	Seraphim	ShRPYM	Fiery Serpents
6	Melekim, Shinanim	MLKYM, ShNANYM	Kings, Ivory Ones
7	Elohim, Tarshishim	ALHYM, ThRShYShYM	Gods, Topazes
8	Beni Elohim	BNY ALHYM	Sons of the Gods
9	Kerubim	KRVBYM	Winged Bulls
10	Eshim	AShYM	Flames

9(a) — THE HEBREW ALPHABET

Path	Letter	Name	Transliteration	Meaning	Value
11	א	Aleph	A	Ox	1
12	ב	Beth	B	House	2
13	ג	Gimel	G	Camel	3
14	ד	Daleth	D	Door	4
15	ה	Heh	H	Window	5
16	ו	Vau	V	Nail	6
17	ז	Zayin	Z	Sword	7

Correspondences

18	ח	Cheth	Ch	Fence	8
19	ט	Teth	T	Serpent	9
20	י	Yod	Y	Hand	10
21	כ	Kaph	K	Palm of Hand	20
	ך	Final Kaph			500
22	ל	Lamed	L	Lash	30
23	מ	Mem	M	Water	40
	ם	Final Mem			600
24	נ	Nun	N	Fish	50
	ן	Final Nun			700
25	ס	Samekh	S	Support	60
26	ע	Ayin	O	Eye	70
27	פ	Peh	P	Mouth	80
	ף	Final Peh			800
28	צ	Tzaddi	Tz	Fish-hook	90
	ץ	Final Tzaddi			900
29	ק	Qoph	Q	Back of Head	100
30	ר	Resh	R	Head	200
31	ש	Shin	Sh	Tooth	300
32	ת	Tau	Th	Identifying Mark	400

9(b) — INFLUENCES ON THE ALPHABETIC PATHS

Path	Influence	Hebrew name	Transliteration	Literal meaning
11	Air	Ruach	RVCh	Breath
12	Mercury	Kokab	KVKB	The Star
13	Moon	Levanah	LBNH	Whiteness
14	Venus	Nogah	NVGH	Brightness
15	Aries	Teleh	TLH	Lamb
16	Taurus	Shor	ShVR	Bull
17	Gemini	Teomim	ThAVMYM	Twins
18	Cancer	Sarton	SRTN	Crab
19	Leo	Ari	ARYH	Lion
20	Virgo	Betulah	BThVLH	Maiden

21	Jupiter	Tzedeq	TzDQ	The Righteous
22	Libra	Mazanim	MAZNYM	Balance
23	Water	Maim	MYM	Water
24	Scorpio	Akrab	OQRB	Scorpion
25	Sagittarius	Qashat	QShTh	Bow
26	Capricorn	Gedi	GDY	Kid
27	Mars	Madim	MDYM	Garment
28	Aquarius	Deli	DLY	Bucket
29	Pisces	Dagim	DGYM	Fishes
30	Sun	Shemesh	ShMSh	Sun
31	Fire	Esh	ASh	Fire
32	Saturn	Shabbathai	ShBThAY	The Restful

10 — ARCHANGELS OF THE 32 PATHS

Path	Archangel	Transliteration	Meaning
1	Metatron	MTTRVN	Visiting the Throne
2	Ratziel	RTzYAL	Will of God
3	Tzaphqiel	TzPQYAL	Watchtower of God
4	Tzadqiel	TzDQYAL	Righteousness of God
5	Kamael	KMAL	Desired (or Treasure) of God
6	Raphael	RPAL	Deliverance of God
7	Haniel	HANYAL	Look to God
8	Michael	MYKAL	Who is like to God
9	Gabriel	GBRYAL	Strength of God
10	Sandalphon	SNDLPVN	The Dew is Poured Forth
11	Raphael	*as 6 above*	*as 6 above*
12	Michael	*as 8 above*	*as 8 above*
13	Gabriel	*as 9 above*	*as 9 above*
14	Haniel	*as 7 above*	*as 7 above*
15	Melkidael	MLKYDAL	Kingship of God
16	Asmodel	ASMVDAL	Harvests of God
17	Ambriel	AMBRYAL	Fortified City of God
18	Muriel	MVRYAL	Threshing of God
19	Arkiel	ORKYAL	God disposes
20	Hamaliel	HMLYAL	Patience of God

21	Tzadqiel	*as 4 above*	*as 4 above*
22	Zuniel	ZVNYAL	God nourishes
23	Gabriel	*as 9 above*	*as 9 above*
24	Berakiel	BRKYAL	Blessing of God
25	Adukiel	ADVKYAL	Fine Grinding of God
26	Hanael	HNAL	Favour of God
27	Kamael	*as 5 above*	*as 5 above*
28	Kambriel	KMBRYAL	Champion of God
29	Amnitziel	AMNYTzYAL	Born of the Covenant of God
30	Raphael	*as 6 above*	*as 6 above*
31	Michael	*as 8 above*	*as 8 above*
32	Tzaphqiel	*as 3 above*	*as 3 above*

11 — ANGELS OF THE ALPHABETIC PATHS

Path	Angel	Transliteration	Meaning
11	Chassan	ChShN	The Breastplate
12	Raphael	RPAL	Deliverance of God
13	Gabriel	GBRYAL	Strength of God
14	Anael	ONAL	Reply of God
15	Sharhiel	ShRHYAL	Armour of God
16	Araziel	ARZYAL	Cedar of God
17	Sarayel	SRAYAL	Liberty of God
18	Pekiel	PKYAL	Pitcher of God
19	Sheratiel	ShRTYAL	Chain of God
20	Shelathiel	ShLThYAL	God gives Comfort
21	Sachiel	SChYAL	Divine Outpouring
22	Chedeqiel	ChDQYAL	Thorn of God
23	Taliahad	TLYHD	The One Adornment
24	Saitziel	SAYTzYAL	God has regarded his child
25	Saritiel	SRYTYAL	Authority of God
26	Mequriel	MQVRYAL	Wellspring of God
27	Zamael	ZMAL	God has determined
28	Tzaqmeqiel	TzQMQYAL	God has poured out as a fountain
29	Nakabiel	NKBYAL	Made plenteous by God

30	Michael	MKYAL	Who is like to God
31	Aral	ARAL	Lion of God
32	Cassiel	KSYAL	Fool of God

12 — INCENSES, PERFUMES, BOTANICAL SYMBOLS

Path	Materials
3	Myrrh. Jet. Guaiac wood (lignum vitae). Oil of violet. Violet leaves, dried. Poppy heads. Cypress.
4	Resin of pine. Copal. Olive: wood, oil. Cedar: wood, oil. Nutmeg.
5	Opoponax. Dragons blood. Aloes wood. Oil of nicotiana. Oil of peppermint. Oil of spearmint. Ginger: root and stem.
6	Olibanum (Frankincense). Heliotropin. Gum arabic. Sun flower oil. Cinnamon bark. Acacia: wood, leaves. Laurel: berries, dried leaves. Angelica: stems, flowers, dried leaves. Vanilla: pods, essence.
7	Benzoin of Sumatra. Red Storax. Young amber. Saffron stamens. Red sandalwood. Oil of verbena. Oil of roses. Tincture of ambergris.
8	Mastic. Liquid storax (*Liquidambar*). Spikenard: oil (for Hermes Psychopompos). Lavender: flowers, oil. Yellow sandal: wood, oil.
9	Camphor. Galbanum. Terebinth: wood, oil. Hazel: wood, nuts. Bay leaves. Lemon verbena leaves, dried. Florentine iris, root. All aromatic seeds. Melon seeds. Marrow seeds. Oil of jasmine (for astral travelling).
10	Asafoetida: gum, grass. All fruit woods, and their exuded gum. Fragrant grasses, flowering reeds. Ivy: berries, leaves. Dittany (for materialisations).
11	Almond oil. Lilac and other types of syringa: wood, flowers. White anemone in flower. Pelargonium: growing plant, flower.
12	Mastic. Star anise. Fennel: oil, dried leaves. Herbs of genus *Mercurialis*.
13	Galbanum. Aromatic extracts from all liliaceous plants. Bay leaves. Lemon verbena leaves, dried.
14	Siamese benzoin. Rose buds, dried. Myrtle: wood, dried

leaves, flowers.
15 Dragons blood. Oil of mustard. Capucine (*nasturtium*): dried seeds and leaves, flowers. Arnica, all species.
16 Red Storax. Wood of box-tree. Caltha.
17 Mistletoe, dried. Walnut: nut, oil. Freezia: flowers. White lavender.
18 Coco palm: nut, oil. Seaweed, dried. Hawthorn.
19 Frankincense. Sunflower: seeds, oil. Marigold (all kinds): flowers.
20 Liquid storax. Narcissus: flowers, oil. White trumpet lily. Fern (all kinds): dried fronds.
21 Copal. Cedar: wood, oil. Olive: wood, oil. Nutmeg. Mountain ash.
22 Galbanum. Geranium: oil, dried leaves.
23 Myrrh. Willow: wood, dried leaves. Rosemary: oil, leaves. Blue lotus. Iris.
24 Spikenard. Cassia: oil, buds. Patchouli. Bistort: root, dried.
25 Cedar: wood, oil. Aloes wood. Balsam of Peru.
26 Cumin. Ginseng. Wormwood.
27 Cloves: buds, oil. Peppercorns, crushed. Solomon's seal (*Polygonata*): flowers.
28 Tincture of ambergris. Night-scented stock.
29 Myrrh. *Scutellaria*: flowers, dried. Lily of the Valley: flowers, perfume.
30 Beeswax. Frankincense. Heliotrope: oil, flowers. Laurel: berries, leaves.
31 Mustard: seeds, oil. Burgundy pitch. Corozo nut. Brazil nut. Dragons blood.
32 Jet. Gum tragacanth. Rue: dried leaves. Cypress: wood, leaves. Oil of Violet. Poppy.

13 — GEMSTONES AND OTHER MINERALS

Path Materials
1 Diamond.
2 Ruby. Lapis lazuli.
3 Sapphire (deep blue). Onyx. Pearl (white, grey). Dark granite with inclusions of mica. Lead crystal. Galena.
4 Amethyst. Sapphire (bright blue). Bluejohn. Labradorite.

	Lapis lazuli.
5	Ruby. Garnet. Red agate. Iron pyrites.
6	Topaz. Zircon (white or blue). Rose quartz. Crysoleth.
7	Emerald. Malachite. Amber (fossil).
8	Opal. Banded agate. Alexandrite. Cinnabar. Abalone shell. Rhinestone.
9	Moonstone. Rock crystal. Fluorspar. Lapis lazuli.
10	Moss agate. Lignite. Pearl (black). Multi-coloured marble. Glass prism.
11	Lodestone. Alabaster. Rock crystal. Coloured glass.
12	Opal. Hyacinth (jacinth). Tourmaline.
13	Moonstone. Hyalite.
14	Emerald. Rose jade. Amber (fossil).
15	Marcasite. All spiral crystals. Red jasper.
16	Carnelian. Green jasper. Steatite.
17	Iceland spar. Shell cameos.
18	Selenium. Skeleton of sea-urchin (fossil). Crafted scarabs of stone or faience. Fossil trilobite.
19	All chatoyant stones. Topaz (yellow). Beryl (yellow).
20	Jade (green, white). Feldspar. Peridot.
21	Amethyst. Lapis lazuli. Bluejohn. Labradorite.
22	Pearl (rose). Malachite (equally banded light and dark).
23	Aquamarine. Beryl (pale green). Pearl (white). Mother-of-pearl.
24	Obsidian. Bloodstone. Serpentine.
25	Turquoise (blue). Amethyst (deep violet). Topaz (golden). Zircon.
26	Topaz (smoky). Opal (black). All stones with concentric bands.
27	Meteoric rock. Garnet. Iron pyrites. Volcanic rock.
28	Geodes. Blister pearls. Fossil amber with winged inclusions.
29	Baroque pearls. Sapphire (pale). Amethyst matrix.
30	Hyacinth (jacinth). Topaz (yellow, golden). Crysoleth.
31	Flint. Red marble. Red jasper.
32	Black marble. Onyx.

NOTES ON THE CORRESPONDENCES

1 — THE TEN SEPHIROTH

Sephiroth — feminine plural noun, literally meaning "those things which are numbered": related to SPR, "enumeration", as in 2 Chronicles 2:17. All ten Sephiroth are equal to one another in holiness, in perfection, and in necessity to the Divine Purpose.

1. **Kether**, the Crown — On the Way of Emanation, Kether is the precious crown, the "fount of honour" from which radiates all else in our universe. On the Way of Return, Kether is "the end which crowns the work".
2. **Chokmah** — The male, active Wisdom.
3. **Binah** — The female, formative Wisdom.
4. **Chesed**, **Gedulah** — Since it has been impossible to find in Hebrew any one word which adequately conveys the essential quality of the fourth Sephirah in all its might and tenderness, it is hopeless to make the attempt in any language. These two traditional titles are equal in authority and are both indispensable.
5. **Geburah** — "Strength" with no implicit connotation of violence or cruelty.
6. **Tiphareth** — This Sephirah is the central Unity of the Tree of Life. It represents a summation and balance of the Sephiroth which lie above it, and a blending and transmission of their influences, with its own, to the Sephiroth which lie below it. It can also be interpreted as (so to put it) an intelligible reflection of Kether.
7. **Netzach** — Spontaneous, impelling and invincible energy.
8. **Hod** — The self-luminous clarity of directing thought.
9. **Yesod** — The vital ordering and creative focusing of gathered influences.
10. **Malkuth** — In its own manner Malkuth is the summation of all the sephirothic influences. It is in a deep sense our "inheritance", for our earthly life, while by no means satisfying our aspirations, yet endows us with images, concepts and a vocabulary with which to make mental play with our perceptions of higher matters.

2 — SEPHIROTHIC DIVINE NAMES

Explanations and comments on the names and on their meanings are given in Chapter 8. The divine names listed in table 2 of the correspondences are the principal or key names for the Sephiroth. The alternatives and amplified forms which are given in the chapter are set forth here for convenient reference.

Path	Name	Transliteration	Meaning
1	Ehyeh Asher Ehyeh	AHYH AShR AHYH	I am that which I am
2	Abba	ABBA	Father
3	Elohim Chiim	ALHYM ChYYM	Living Elohim
	Aima Elohim	AYMA ALHYM	Bright Mother Elohim
4	El Gedul	AL GDVL	The High God
5	Elohim	ALHYM	Divinity
6	Ha-Qadosh	H-QDSh	The Holy One
	Chai Aulomim	ChY OVLMIM	Life of the Worlds
8	Elohi Qedem	ALHY QDM	Prototypic God
	Elohim Emeth	ALHYM AMTh	God of Truth
9	Shaddai	ShDY	All-Mover
	El Chai	AL ChY	The Living God
10	Adonai Melekh	ADNY MLK	Lord and King
	Adonai ha-Aretz	ADNI H-ARTz	Lord of the World
	Adon kol ha-Aretz	ADN KL H-ARTz	Lord of the whole World

3 — PLANETARY COLOURS AND METALS

The spectrum colours — While the colours of the rainbow have always been regarded as mystically significant, it has only been possible to give planetary attributions to them since research on the spectrum has identified them definitively as seven in number. In practice the allocations seem to sit very easily.

The attribution of the whole *spectrum of seven colours* to Malkuth and to planet Earth is solidly based upon the Qabalistic tradition which attributes the rainbow to the Shekinah. There are manyreferences to this in the Zohar, although the number of colours is there variously reckoned. An alternative ascription of <u>four colours</u>

to Malkuth emphasises the elemental aspects of the sphere of Earth, the colours then being green, blue, red and yellow; or black, russet, olive and pale yellow.

The Ptolemaic colours — Dating from the 2nd century A.D. this system was generally accepted throughout the western world for about 1700 years and still provides useful alternatives or matters for consideration for the magical student. *Gold, nacre, silver* — not only the colour in the strict sense but also the lustre of the material itself is implied in these instances. Saffron is attributed to Venus not only as a colour but also as the substance itself.

Considerations on the planetary metals — Our word "metal" comes to us straight out of the Arabic. In that language MTL means, explicitly, forged iron. This consideration brings a hint of adaptability into our view of the magical metals and, indeed, of all the correspondences.

The seven traditional planetary metals are lead, tin, iron, gold, copper, quicksilver and silver.

3. As the metal of Saturn, lead is admittedly unsurpassed. It is unfortunately no longer the "common substance easily obtained" that it was through many centuries, but its dull lustre and massive density still make it the perfect representative among metals of the accepted Saturnian qualities.

    It has, besides, certain Saturnian qualities to recommend it which (we must presume) were not anciently known. One of these qualities is its resistance to radiation. The other characteristic links it in a curious way to the perceptions of the alchemists.

    To transmute lead, rather than any other substance, into gold has for long been regarded as the most notable achievement in practical alchemy. This is not only because it involves changing the most dull and earthy of metals into the most precious and glorious. It is also because this, above all other transmutations, symbolises and in a sense demonstrates the validity of the spiritual alchemy which achieves the true plenitude of human nature: which transmutes the man of earth, limited to sense-perception and to laborious mental processes, into the perfect and integrated being, illuminated by its higher self and splendid in its faculties.

On the material level, the inner structure of atoms having become technologically accessible for examination, it has been established that a close affinity exists between the atoms of lead and those of gold: an affinity so pronounced that the removal by bombardment of certain electrons from atoms of lead would result, as a physical fact, in their conversion into atoms of gold.

4. Tin was originally considered worthy to be the metal of Jupiter because of its whiteness — the Jupiterian colour in the Ptolemaic scheme — and because of its freedom from corrosion. It now has a relative scarcity which brings it even nearer to qualification as a precious metal. Curiously, the crystals of pure tin are cubic, this giving another justification for the ascription of this metal to the planet which we associate with the fourth Sephirah.

   To obtain, or make, implements of pure tin for use in a rite of Jupiter or Chesed might be a matter of considerable difficulty. However, various types of pewter, which is an alloy of tin with lead and often with additional metals such as silver, are to be commended. These alloys look good, can be delicately worked and are easily kept from tarnishing, and have a further affinity with the sphere of Jupiter in that they are most often employed to make drinking vessels.

5. The positive qualities which once made pure iron the desirable representative of this sphere — its rough strength and the red stain of its rust — were offset by many disadvantages. Now however a great number of admirable steels have been created, so that not only the warrior and the surgeon but the householder, the craftsman and the designer of fine metalwork can appreciate them and make good use of them. It is to be remembered that Hephaestos as well as Mars or Ares is a deity of this Sphere.

6. For "imperishable gold" there is no true substitute. But it may be necessary for many purposes to accept such other yellow metals as the jeweller or the foundry can supply, and some of these metals have a beauty of their own.

7. The warm flesh colour, the tender lustre, the malleable quality of pure copper are all well suited to the character both of the goddess and of the forces of the Sphere. The readiness of the metal to conduct heat or electricity seems related, also, to the swift response of the Venusian nature to the tides and currents of life. And the rocky ores of copper, and even the corrosion of the metal itself, are green as if they took their colour from grove and garden.

8. Quicksilver, even if difficult to obtain, is still with us; but here we can notice thankfully that this age has provided us with other options.

    Certainly in the alchemical context quicksilver admits of no alternative; but generally in the magical environment the great density and curious dry fluidity of quicksilver put it out of series with the other metals and make it unfit for many purposes. Except in a vessel, it cannot be carried, or raised to give authority to a gesture, or inscribed with word or sign.

    As an alternative a metal is required which is pale in colour, light in weight, able to be touched, inscribed and wielded, and which of its very nature and purpose is dedicated to the god of the winged staff and sandals. Here, a light aluminium alloy may be chosen, of a type such as is produced for use in aircraft. The fact that the metal is an alloy would also have relevance, for diversity of qualities belongs to this Sphere.

9. Silver is the chief metal of the Moon. Its sole defects are its ready inclination to tarnish, and its liability unless carefully protected to be permanently blemished by contact with such substances as salt. But its delicate beauty rewards care, and its very defects are characteristic of the Sphere. The brightness of the silver needs to be as carefully guarded as chastity; but do what we will, it is ever by nature changeful as the countenance of Luna.

4 — THE HEAVENS OF ASSIAH

Each of the Sephiroth has assigned to it as one of its symbols some particular heavenly body or phenomenon in the World of Assiah.

To contemplate these symbols in their natural splendour can bring refreshment and a renewed sense of wonder to the soul and frequently, also, enlightenment to the mind.

1. **Rashith ha-Gilgalim** — the "primal whirlings". The Hebrew word GLGLYM signifies "wheels", "circlings", or "whirlwinds". The concept is thus of dynamic revolutions, with connotations of air.

    A cosmic counterpart suggested to the mind is that of a spiral galaxy. The human eye can just perceive the spiral galaxy in Andromeda as a haze of light, but astronomy can provide awesome photographs of the greatness and beauty of this and other celestial phenomena of the kind.

    Thrilling though these images are to contemplate, they can show forth for us only a particular aspect of Kether, not a complete concept of Kether itself. To look upon them however, and to reflect upon the significance of the title "the primal whirlings", is to evoke in the imagination an awareness of that Holy One who has emanated the vast concourse of powers throughout the Worlds, and who ever sustains, from level to level of their being, their interplay of lights and energies, of measured movements and of mighty potencies.

2. **Mazloth** — The cosmic symbol of Chokmah, although still remote from us, is less so than that of Kether. Traditionally Chokmah is represented by the Zodiac, the belt of the heavens which extends about eight degrees on each side of the path of the Sun, and is divided into the familiar twelve Signs.

    The Hebrew name for the Zodiac is *Mazloth*, "the Allocations" or "the Destinies". The zodiacal signs do not represent destiny in any ultimate spiritual sense, but simply indicate the allotment of outward circumstances and inward talents; on this the Zoharic commentary on Genesis quotes a saying to the effect that the good things of life are not rewards of merit, but results of *mazzal*. A person's *mazzal*, then, or "luck", is that which "flows to" him, or "girds" him, for the Hebrew word can be interpreted to mean either "a flowing stream" or "a belt".

    There exists some confusion of root words. In 2 Kings 23:5 the word *mazloth* distinctly means "the planetary powers" in contrast to "all the host of heaven" which would be the stellar powers. The use of this word to mean the Zodiac may have been through association with *Mazroth* (transliterated MZRVTh), "a constellation", or, better to the present context, another form of *Mazroth* (transliterated MAZRVTh), "a belt". In the usage of the Qabalah however, the word *Mazloth* is established as the name of the cosmic symbol of Chokmah..

Chokmah is also properly symbolised by the entire concourse of the hosts of heaven, the gleaming wonder of stars innumerable, the clusters and garlands of quivering light, the nascent stardust gleaming in measureless distances of space.

The host of the stars however, that pulsing and scintillating brilliance, tremendous in beauty and extent, overwhelming in silent power: that is not only the glory of Chokmah, it is the glory also of Binah. They are inseparable even as the night sky is inseparable from its teeming multitude of stars. For the immeasurable velvet darkness of the Mother's womb gives birth to the light of the Father's star-seed, even as his unseen dynamism gives life to her ever-wondrous, conceptualising mystery. Whether in our contemplation of their glorious symbols, or in the mystic reality which the mind seeks in awe to approach, each of these Supernals, Chokmah and Binah, makes revelation of the grandeur of the other.

3. **Shabbathai** — The symbol of Binah at the planetary level of the Sephirah is Saturn. The association of the Hebrew name *Shabbathai* with the Sabbath is evident but, on account of the meaning of the name ("rest" or "termination") the planet is often associated traditionally with influences of hindrance, opposition and death. At a deeper level however, Saturn represents the great forces of transformation, renewal and regeneration. In the astrology of the Renaissance, Saturn was recognised as the planet especially of the creative artist, inspiring and empowering him to transform his materials into things of new meaning, purpose and beauty.

6. **Shemesh** — The general Semitic name for the sun, whether personalised or as simply "the light of the Sun". The Sun

represents for us pure energy, as it were fixed in time and space, giving boundlessly of itself to provide life-giving heat and light to all beings. Thus contemplated in relation to our physical existence and then in more spiritual aspects, the Sun and the inner force represented by the Sun have through the ages received the worship and adoration of countless peoples. The resolve of Geburah, the magnificence of Chesed and the spiritual force of supernal light are gathered together for us in the golden beauty of Tiphareth, whose symbol in Assiah we in our turn may reverence.

7. **Nogah** — The wonderful brilliancy of the planet Venus, the symbol in Assiah of Netzach, is unique in our Solar System. Physically, the effect is caused by sunlight reflected from the dense cloud which perpetually mantles the planet. Considered in this context, the title of the Yetziratic Heaven of Netzach, *Shechaqim*, "Clouds", leads to some interesting speculations.

8. **Kokab** — Mercury is "the Star", as a unique title.

10. **Cholem Yesodoth** — The Sphere of the Elements, Fire, Air, Water and Earth; in other words, the material world in which we live.

   The planet Earth is for us a material symbol of the Sephirah Malkuth. All the imagery and interaction of the world of Nature is open before us in its mystery and beauty for our contemplation, and for our further reflection by inference and analogy upon the greater mysteries and the more sublime beauty which lie beyond.

   The heavenly bodies representing the other planetary Sephiroth are visible as distant objects of wonder; but Malkuth too has its particular Assiatic "sign in the heavens". For this Sephirah is the special domain of the Shekinah, who among her titles is known as the Mistress and the King's Daughter. And sacred to the greatly revered Shekinah is the rainbow.

   The rainbow, so the Zoharic commentary on Genesis tells us, is not only the sign of the covenant between God and man which is indicated in the story of Noah. It is the very likeness of the radiance with which the Shekinah appears. The Zohar here cites Ezekiel 1:28 — "As the appearance of the bow that is in the cloud in the day of rain, so was the appearance of the brightness round about."

There is yet another reason for the association of the rainbow with Malkuth. Although the mediaevals had no exact knowledge of the spectrum — they did not, for example, discern the band of indigo — they nevertheless conceived of the colours as symbolic of the influences reflected upon Malkuth from the other Sephiroth. It is suggested in the Zohar that these reflected colours appear as flowers upon the Earth: that they are brought, in fact, into the very life of Earth.

5 — THE SEVEN HEAVENS OF YETZIRAH

1, 2, 3, **Araboth** — Sometimes ORBTh, with the same pronunciation. In other contexts this word would mean "deserts". However, the imageless Heaven of the Supernals suggests the translation of "plains".

The word occurs in Psalm 68:4, "Extol him who rides upon the Araboth," that is, upon the highest Heaven. There is a curious reference to this in the Zoharic commentary on Exodus, which explicitly identifies the Araboth by proceeding with this interpretation: "Be glad in the presence of him who rides upon that concealed Heaven which is supported by the Chayoth". At the same time, this Zoharic passage also interprets the word Araboth to mean "mixture" because — it says — this Heaven is a mixture of fire and water.

There is indeed a word ORB meaning "mixed". It does not affect the meaning of Araboth; however, such a tradition may well be connected with the description in the Book of Revelation, 15:2, "as it were a sea of glass mixed with fire."

4. **Makon** — A Jupiterian sense of changeless prosperity is implied.

5. **Ma'on** — Of several interpretations, that of "a refuge" is chosen as most suited to denote the Heaven of Geburah.

6. **Zebul** — The word means simply "habitation". But there is an implication here of "a sure habitation" by Qabalistic reasoning. This is the Heaven of the sixth Sephirah; and Zebulun, the sixth

son of Leah, was given his name as being the guarantee of her secure position. (Genesis 30:20).

7. **Shechaqim** — The image of "cloud" as the garment of mystery; but this is also a heaven which is "a fountain of gardens and a well of living waters".

8. **Reqia** — This "expanse" may be externally conceived of as a golden canopy. Inwardly, spiritually, it is composed of innumerable and wondrous dwellings.

10. **Vilon** — Sometimes given as **Vilon Shemaim**, "Veil of the Heavens".

6 — THE SEVEN HELLS

1, 2, 3. **Sheol** — The name given to the deepest Hell, corresponding to the height of the Supernals. In ancient times Sheol was the name of the Great Mother in her aspect as the devouring Queen of the Underworld: hence its supernal attribution. The literal meaning of the name is "she who is implored in prayer". Comparably to the Greek Hades, the name was in later times transferred from the deity to the region.

4. **Abaddon** — The simple Hebrew meaning of the word is "destruction". In time this appears to have been influenced by the Greek *abyssos,* "bottomless pit", probably also by the Egyptian *Abtu* (Abydos), principal seat of the worship of Osiris as lord of the realm of death.

5, 6, 7. **Bar-Schachath**, **Tit ha-Yeven**, **Shaare-Maveth** — Simple Hebrew phrases. Shaare-Maveth is sometimes rendered "Gate of the Grave".

8. **Tzal-Maveth** — "Shadow of Death". This title is used in the famous passage of Psalm 23: "through the valley of the shadow of death": B-GYA TzLMVTh, the word gi (GY) signifying a deep rift or gully.

9. **Gi-Hinnom** — Also called Gehenna, this ravine was from time immemorial the repository of all the refuse of the city of Jerusalem. It also provided a mass grave and a place of cremation for the corpses of the destitute and of those put to death as criminals. As a typical application of this image, the Zoharic commentary on Genesis has: "the angels who rebelled and who were annihilated by the fire of Gi-Hinnom."

7 — THE SEVEN PALACES IN BRIAH

On its emanation from Atziluth into Briah, the essential nature of a Sephirah extends outwards from itself in Briah a pure light which enfolds it, forming a "vesture". This "vesture" is the Briatic "Palace" of the Sephirah.

1, 2, 3. **Hekel Qadosh Qadeshim** - The title of the Palace of the Supernals indicates its transcendence of any experience which could be described in earthly terms. It is "the Life of the Worlds". But the next note sets it in a less inaccessible light.

4. **Hekel Ahabah** (or **Ahbah**) — The Zoharic commentary on Exodus states that the four letters *Aleph, Heh, Beth, Heh* dispose all things in perfect unity, and thus form a chariot in which to mount to the supernal heights.

    This passage expresses true Qabalistic teaching upon the mystical power of AHBH, love. But gematria throws further light upon the matter. It can be observed that the numerical total of AHBH is 13. *Merkabah,* chariot, is transliterated as MRKBH which gives 267. Now, $13 + 267 = 280$. This reduces to 28, and 28 is a "perfect" number. (A "perfect" number is the sum of all its divisors: in this case, $1 + 2 + 4 + 7 + 14 = 28$.) When AHBH has reached the supernal height however, it finds itself again; for the sum of *Kether* KThR (620), *Chokmah* ChKMH (73) and *Binah* BYNH (67) is 760, and 760 reduces to 13, the number of AHBH.

5, 6. **Hekel Zakuth, Hekel Ratzon** — The names of these Palaces are well and clearly suited to the Sephiroth which they represent.

7. **Hekel Etzem Shemaim** — "The Palace of the Essence of the Heavens" could also be rendered as "the very heaven of heavens". This, the Palace of Netzach, is the blissful apotheosis of the world of Nature and of the faculties by which the psyche delights in it.

8. **Hekel Thushiah** — The name of this Palace can have several shades of meaning, all of which are associated with the various gifts of Hod: material gain, security, wisdom. This Palace is frequently called **Hekel Gonah** (HKL GVNH), "Palace of Serenity", a title perhaps implying philosophic calm, but somewhat less apposite than could be desired for the magical vitality of Hod.

9, 10. **Hekel Garen ha-Saphir** — Otherwise given as **Hekel Labanath ha-Saphir**, "Palace of the Tiles (that is, pavement) of Lapis". SPYR is not the precious transparent sapphire, which was unknown in ancient times: it is lapis lazuli, and its mention in this context is comparable to that in the vision of Ezekiel.

8 — THE SEPHIROTHIC CHORAS OF ANGELS

1. **Chayoth ha-Qadesh** — The angels of Kether are the "Holy Living Ones", exalted and pure existences, truly representing the nature of Kether in the angelic world. They should not be confused, in name or in appearance, with the ChYVTh, the "living beings" of Ezekiel's vision, which are specifically Kerubim (see below).

4. **Chashmalim** — From ChShML, "amber". These glorious Shining Ones of Chesed are indicated by their title as appearing in the varied and luminous colours of amber.

    A confusion as to the meaning of the title has sometimes arisen because the Septuagint renders the word ChShML, "amber", as *elektron*. This is the normal Greek name for amber, given in ancient times on account of the magnetic property of the substance; but in later times the same Greek name was given to a brightly lustrous alloy of gold and silver. However, either interpretation pays tribute to the brilliant glory of the Chashmalim.

5. **Seraphim** — The title of this chora is sometimes given as "The Burning Ones", deriving the name from SRP, "to burn". They are properly, however, the "Serpents of Fire", a title which may relate their traditional function as communicators between heaven and earth to the image of the lightnings. In their aspect as heralds of the divine glory, they are imaged as "the six-winged Seraphs" of Ezekiel's vision (Ezekiel 6:2).

6, 7. **Melekim/Shinanim, Elohim/Tarshishim** — Two currents of tradition are here represented in respect of Tiphareth and Netzach. In each case the more widely adopted name is given first.

8. **Beni Elohim** — "Sons of the Gods". This title of the chora of Hod implies a definite relationship to the chora of Netzach, one of the titles of which is "the Gods". It may be observed here that the energies of Hod, in association with those of Netzach, are truly dynamic and magical; but that isolated from the vitality of Netzach, the activity of Hod degenerates into passive intellectualism and sterile formality.

9. **Kerubim** — The mysterious Kerubim are guardians and avengers. They are implacable, silent and awesome. As ministers of the Holy One, they form a "throne" upon which the Glory of his Presence rests, or a chariot upon which he rides; and with their shadowing wings they veil the splendour of the godhead.

Their traditional and ancient form is that of "Winged Bulls". But their appearance may vary according to the specific divine attributes they manifest. Thus they sometimes appear as human-headed winged bulls, comparable to those of Assyrian sculpture. They may appear also in human form, with two or four wings, and with one, two or four faces. The four faces are specified in Ezekiel 1:10 as *man, lion, ox* and *eagle*; so that Ezekiel 10:14, in making reference to the faces as those of *kerub, man, lion* and *eagle*, corroborates the primal evidence of bovine imagery in respect of the kerubim.

9(a), 9(b) — THE HEBREW ALPHABET and INFLUENCES ON THE ALPHABETIC PATHS

11. **Aleph** — א — Originally a simple vertical like the Arabic *Alif*, this letter has become distinguished by the addition of "wings". In venerable Hebrew books illuminated on parchment, an initial *Aleph* is sometimes found elaborated into the shape of a flying bird. The ascription of Elemental Air to this Path is well recognized.

12. **Beth** — ב — The house stands on a level platform; its front is open to the left. If *Aleph* implies radiant spirituality, *Beth* implies containment and the ordering of energies.

13. **Gimel** — ג — Both this letter and the camel whose shape it represents call to mind the crescent moon which traverses the trackless space of the heavens, even as Gimel covers the long Path from Tiphareth to Kether.

17. **Zayin** — ז — Gemini seen as "one divided" rather than as "two united".

18. **Cheth** — ח — "Fence"; or "enclosed" as the crab is in its shell.

19. **Teth** — ט — The serpent of this letter is curled head to tail.

20. **Yod** — י — The potency-latency of this letter is curiously illustrated by its history in modern mathematics, which culminates in its establishment as the decimal point.

21. **Kaph** — כ ך — The palm of this hand has the power and the liberality of Jupiter to hold and to bestow: *Kaph* is the "cupped hand", *final Kaph* the "open hand."

24. **Nun** — נ ן — The usual word for "fish" is *dag*, DG. Nun implies essentially an elongated creature. In the context of the sign of Scorpio, which is of the Triplicity of Water, it even suggests a water-snake.

26. **Ayin** — ע — If turned on its left side, the letter represents an eye drawn in a style which resembles the Egyptian. The word *Ayin*, OYN, likewise means "eye", but also has the meaning of a spring, fountain or well. In esoteric thought these meanings are often blended, in the image of insatiable gazing (Ecclesiastes 1:8) and of sight as a wellspring of creativity. *Gedi* signifies the kid, not the adult goat.

29. **Qoph** — ק — The letter represents neck and cranium without the face.

30. **Resh** — ר — The "head" here emphatically implies the glorious face of the Sun.

31. **Shin** — ש — This three-pronged letter is interpreted as a tooth. As the influence upon the Path is elemental Fire, the tooth may be seen as specifically a flame of that devouring element.

32. **Tau** — ת — By tradition the simple form of the "Tau Cross" is the original "identifying mark" signified by this letter. By tradition also, this sign is implied in Exodus 12:7 and in Genesis 4:15 as being used for the Saturnian purpose of preserving the life of the persons concerned in those episodes.

10 — ARCHANGELS OF THE 32 PATHS

1. **Metatron** — Taking the name to be Greek, it can be translated literally as "Visiting the Throne", which accords well with the traditional interpretation, "Messenger of the Divine Presence". As the power more exalted than any other being of angelic nature, Metatron is called "Ruler of the Princes".

6. **Raphael** — This name is frequently rendered as "Healing of God" but the scope of powers indicated in the Hebrew is wider and implies liberation at every level.

10. **Sandalphon** — The "dew" which is here poured forth is understood to be the blessing or influence of God.

16, 18. **Asmodel, Muriel** — The meanings of these two names balance one another, upon the Columns of Mercy and Severity respectively.

22. **Zuniel** — Otherwise given as *Zuriel*. The letter ascribed to this Path, Lamed, signifies "the lash", but the ruling planet of the sign Libra is Venus. Path 22 thus indicates a balance between severity and mercy: Zuniel, archangel of abundance, brings reward out of toil.

25. **Adukiel** — This name takes a metaphor from the milling of grain. In the evolutionary journey, the 25th Path leads from Yesod in Yetzirah to Tiphareth in Briah. The rough materials in the Nephesh must be milled out of the personality for this transition.

11 — ANGELS OF THE ALPHABETIC PATHS

11. **Chassan** — This word signifies a richly adorned breastplate, suitable to ceremonial use and typified by that of the High Priest. The name is appropriate to the angel of Air because the breastplate protects the thorax.

12. **Raphael** — Not to be confused with the archangel of Tiphareth. Some names, while expressing a certain general character, can carry different shades of meaning and application, so as to characterise angelic or archangelic beings who may none the less differ in spiritual status, and in sephirothic attribution.

13. **Gabriel** — See the foregoing note concerning the name Raphael.

14. **Anael** — Sometimes the Hebrew form of this name is given incorrectly as ANAL. The name Anael is related to ONN, "(he) practised divination". Games of chance, traditionally ascribed to the Venusian powers, in many cases take their origin from divinatory procedures. The angel of the Sphere of Venus can thus be understood to give response to a divinatory question.

15. **Sharhiel** — This name may represent either ShRHYAL, "Armour of God", or ShRYHAL, "Indignation of God". Either is suitable to the letter Heh and to the Path of Aries.

16. **Araziel** — This Path rises from Chesed, to which the cedar tree corresponds.

17. **Sarayel** — This is the Path of the sign Gemini, which belongs to the Triplicity of Air and has Mercury as its ruling planet. Its angel represents a God-given freedom upon a Path between extremes.

18. **Pekiel** — The literal translation "Pitcher of God" combines the idea of a shell or casing with the idea of the world of waters.

19. **Sheratiel** — This is the Path which links Geburah and Chesed. The name of the angel seems to allude to the looped serpent which forms the letter Teth, but also it indicates a powerful bond — with the strength of the Lion — between the Columns of Severity and Mercy. Strength unites Severity and Mercy where weakness would separate them.

20. **Shelathiel** — The first part of this name, ShL, is related to *Shalom*, "Peace". The meaning of "comfort" which attaches here is supported by the sign Virgo which belongs to the Triplicity of Earth; furthermore, this Path leads from the Column of Equilibrium to the Column of Mercy.

21. **Sachiel** — "Divine Outpouring" or, "Poured out by God". As frequently occurs, the Path of Jupiter is associated with the idea of abundant gifts, poured as it were from the Cornucopia.

22. **Chedeqiel** — This Path, from Tiphareth to Geburah, carries the traveller from sunshine to storm. Also it carries the letter Lamed, "the lash". For the connotation of exactly the kind of thorn which is indicated by the name of this angel, see Proverbs 15:19.

23. **Taliahad** — The 23rd Path lies entirely upon the Column of Severity, the austere way from Hod to Geburah. Because the letter Mem signifies Water and the influence upon the Path is likewise Water (the only instance where the significance of a letter and the influence upon a Path are one and the same), this

Path may truly be said to have but "one adornment".

24. **Saitziel** — Upon this Path "from Victory to Beauty" the traveller passes through the deep waters; but "God has regarded — or 'raised up' — his child".

25. **Saritiel** — This angel is envisaged as a high official with authority to admit the worthy traveller to Tiphareth in Yetzirah. The word SRYS which is part of the root of the name originally meant "a eunuch" but — as often in the annals of oriental government — the title came to indicate high dignity without inference as to the bearer's sexual status.

26. **Mequriel** — The title "Wellspring of God" bespeaks a dynamic source of inspiration appropriate to the sign Capricorn and to the interpretation of Ayin as "a well".

27. **Zamael** — The expressiveness of the letter Peh and the fiery resolve of Mars are well represented in the title "God has determined".

28. **Tzaqmeqiel** — Sometimes the Hebrew form is spelled as TzKMQYAL. The fitness of the meaning of this name for the Path of Aquarius is evident.

29. **Nakabiel** — Sometimes the Hebrew form is given as VKBYAL. The name is associated with God-given plenitude as of a flowing river. This accords with the nature of the sign Pisces and also that of the aquatic aspect of its ruling planet, Jupiter, typified by abundance.

30. **Michael** — See entry 12 above.

31. **Aral** — The name of the angel of elemental Fire, Aral, "Lion of God", was also the name given to the altar of burnt offerings at Jerusalem.

32. **Cassiel** — The meaning of this name has no ambiguity, and invites reflection. Of obvious scriptural references to fools, we

can dismiss the fool who denies God, and likewise the babbling fool who certainly cannot be of a Saturnian nature.

But again, "the fool walks in darkness" (Ecclesiastes 2:14), and the 32nd is a Path of darkness. It is also the Path upon which the greatest wisdom — in which this angel must guide the traveller — is to step forward in that darkness, towards a goal of which the reality is not immediately discernible. The traveller can do this boldly, for at the outset he is the "foolish son" in Malkuth and rashness is in his nature.

12 — INCENSES, PERFUMES, BOTANICAL SYMBOLS

No direction is given as to which materials are intended for each category of use, for many are interchangeable. "Rose" can be interpreted as dried petals for incense or for potpourri, as a rose-scented candle, as a rose placed as emblem upon the altar, etc. Even where a specific use is indicated, adaptations can be made. Moreover, the lists are by no means exclusive. The world of plant life is wide and by nature magical, and many further materials as they may be available can find place here.

3. **Jet** — A fossilised sea-coal traditional to Saturn for its antiquity and colour. Combustible as incense.

4. **Copal** — An incense gum from various South American trees, appropriate to Jupiter for character and aroma. The consonants of its name can be transliterated as KPL = 130, reducing to 4 for the 4th Sepirah.

5. **Dragons Blood** — A small-grained resin which explodes lightly into fiery particles when cast on a fire.

6. **Acacia** — Ancient emblem of regeneration, recognised in Egypt. **Sunflower oil** — A useful modern material. **Angelica** — An exquisite aromatic and demonifuge, a frequent ingredient of communion breads in the mediaeval church.

7. **Young amber** — Resin from conifers of the Baltic region, not fossilised. **Saffron** — An ancient attribute of Venus.

8. **Essential oils** — Besides fragrant oils such as those listed, all healthful and beneficent oils can be ascribed here.

9. **Terebinth** — A lunar fragrance which is more robust than camphor. The name of the tree in Hebrew is ALH which totals 36. **Coriander,** etc. — Any seeds to be used as incense should be slightly cracked, to prevent their possible explosion when heated.

10. **Asafoetida** — A traditional and potent purifier of the lower astral ambience. **Dittany** — The leaves are soft and covered with down: when burned they give off a dense vapour of pleasant odour. Traditional for rites of materialisation.

11. **Syringa** — Chosen for elemental Air, not only because of its fragrant blossoms but also because of the ancient use of its stems for flutes, whence the name *syringa*. **White anemone** — By its name intrinsically ascribed to elemental Air. **Pelargonium** — Grown as an indoor plant it is a natural air-purifier.

12. **Star Anise** — Anise is a characteristic incense of Hod. The star-shaped pods of this variety give it a special affinity to this Path bearing the influence of the planet Mercury, of which the Hebrew name signifies "The Star".

13. **Liliaceous plants** — All are lunar: for their exquisite fragrance certainly, but also because plant and flower (except in certain cultivated varieties) have a basically threefold structure, thus suggesting the 3 phases of the Moon.

14. **Myrtle** — Sacred to Venus-Aphrodite, Goddess of Love. Before orange blossom became traditional for wedding wreaths, the fragrant white blossoms of Myrtle were long dedicated in European countries for that purpose.

15. **Capucine** (Nasturtium) — Appropriate for the varied fiery colours of its flowers and for the peppery flavour of leaves and seeds.

16. **Red storax** — A small-grained resin, appropriate to Venus, the ruling planet of Taurus, for its delicate sweetness. For Taurus specifically, **Caltha** (kingcup) — beloved by the bovine kind.

17. **Mistletoe** — Placed upon this Path for its paired leaves and its preference for aereal abode. **Walnut** — for the nut itself: the divided shell for Gemini, the resemblance of the kernel to a brain for the intellectual character of Gemini's ruling planet Mercury. **White lavender** — for its colour and fragrance, suited to the high aereal nature of Mercury.

18. **Dried seaweed** — The common seaweed called bladder wrack, or one of the fragrant seaweeds, are most suited here as incense materials. **Hawthorn** — The masses of moon-white blossom with their wholly feminine fragrance give one reason for this ascription: another reason, relating to Cheth as "the Fence", is the renowned history of the hawthorn hedge as mighty defence.

19. **Frankincense (Olibanum)** — For its dominating fragrance, and for the golden colour and noble size of its "tears", this has through the ages been the traditional solar offering.

20. **White trumpet lily** — As symbol of virginity.

21. **Mountain Ash** — Appropriate here for its home in the heights, and for the power ascribed to it of turning aside lightning

22. **Geranium** — The musky aroma is appropriate to Venus, the ruling planet of Libra. The leaves of the plant are appropriate to the Sign: they combine the complementary colours, green and red.

23. **Rosemary** — Attributed here because of the Latin name, given both as *ros marinus* and as *ros maris*, meaning "dew of the sea" in each instance. Not only the small blue flowers but the whole plant has in its fragrance something of the tang of the sea.

24. All these perfumes have an overtone of melancholy, but are glorious in their depths. **Spikenard** in particular, apart from its

ancient use in embalming, is associated with the resurgent Phoenix

25. **Balsam of Peru** — A rich, intensely fragrant gum, frequently used as an ingredient in anointing oil, to which even a small amount imparts depth and nobility. The sacerdotal and magical associations of the gum make it a fitting and operative symbol upon the Path of the Archer.

26. **Ginseng** — placed on this Path because of its tonic and euphoric properties. **Wormwood** — also a tonic and stimulant, likewise appropriate.

27. **Cloves, peppercorns** — placed here because they are fiery to the mouth. **Solomon's seal** — plant named on account of its flowers which, like the seal of Solomon, are 5-pointed stars: here appropriate because the number 5 is associated with Mars.

28. **Night-scented stock** — This Path merits fragrance, carrying as it does the fascination of Tzaddi and the airy influence of Aquarius; and night-scented stock, with the nocturnal flood of perfume from its small flowers, evokes also the mystery of Aquarius' traditional ruling planet Saturn and the unexpectedness of Uranus the modern ruler of the Sign.

29. **Scutellaria** — Appropriate for its flowers, which are shaped like a cap or a cranium. Any flower of similar shape would be suitable.

30. **Beeswax** — On account of its hexagonal cells, the number 6 being associated with the Sun. **Laurel** — for its classical association with Apollo.

31. **Corozo nut** — Seed of the South American corozo palm, *Phytelephas macrocarpa*. Given upon this Path with reference to the letter Shin, "a tooth", (or, often, "a tusk"), because as the name *Phytelephas* reveals, the nut has been much employed as vegetable ivory. **Brazil nut** — The kernel can be blanched to resemble a tooth. If set upright and ignited at the tip, it burns

gently like a cone of incense.

32. Resins and other materials of general Saturnian attribution.

13 — GEMSTONES AND OTHER MINERALS

1. **Diamond** — "Immortal diamond" is the only mineral which can be chosen to represent Kether: for its supreme brilliance certainly, but also because all colours are present, as it were potentially, in its prismatic lustre.

2. **Ruby** — For the Yod of Tetragrammaton, the creative flame of the supernal male potency. **Lapis lazuli** — Anciently associated with the celestial father for its deep blue, and for its gold inclusions suggesting stars in the vault of heaven.

3. **Deep blue sapphire** — Representing supernal Binah as the great ocean-mother; but equally as the ocean of infinite space. **Onyx** — The velvet darkness of the stone equally represents the supernal or the planetary aspect of the Sephirah. **Pearl** — For Binah as "fount of forms". **Dark granite**, **lead crystal**, **galena** — For Saturn.

4. **Amethyst** — Traditional gemstone for Chesed-Jupiter. **Bright blue sapphire** — For the sky-father. **Lapis lazuli** — The "sacred lapis" is attributed here as representing both the regality and the priestliness of the Sphere.

5. **Ruby** — Representing the divine energy of Geburah-Mars. **Garnet** — Suitable not only for its red colour but also as the traditional symbol of the strength of loyal friendship. **Red agate** — For victory and for triumph over adversity.

6. **Topaz** — Symbolising the alchemical quintessence, the intrinsic mystery of Tiphareth, and the ennobled human heart. **Zircon** — For the vital radiance of the Sphere. **Rose quartz** — Representing divine ekstasis, the infusion of the heart with the transmuting fire of the godhead. **Crysoleth** — For the solar splendour.

7. **Emerald** — The supreme gemstone of Netzach-Venus. **Malachite** — For its colour and also as being a carbonate of copper. **Fossil amber** — As being carried by the sea (with reference to Anadyomene) and as being frequently close to the colour of saffron. Also for its power of attraction.

8. **Opal, alexandrite, abalone** — All noted for changeable hues. **Cinnabar** — Mercuric oxide of brownish-red or vermilion colour. **Banded agate** — Representing the mercurial duality which is symbolised in the cadeuceus. **Rhinestone** — A synthetic stone, brilliantly scintillating with changeable colours; product of the science and craftsmanship which typify the Sphere of Mercury.

9. **Rock crystal** — Because the mineral receives and holds impressions, and because it retains and focuses astral energies. **Lapis lazuli** — Attributed here for its association with Yesod as the appearance of the throne above the firmament. (Ezekiel 1:26). **Fluorspar** — Given here for its whiteness and for its use in metallurgy to promote fluidity.

10. **Moss agate** — Has a mineral inclusion of dendritic crystals resembling moss in colour and structure. **Lignite** — Fossilised wood showing vegetable structure. **Black pearl** — For its colour, and because "Malkuth sits upon the throne of Binah". **Glass prism** — A wedge-shaped artefact of clear glass, by which a beam of white light can be split into the seven colours of the spectrum: here attributed to Malkuth because the rainbow with its colours is the special and wondrous symbol of the Shekinah.

11. **Lodestone** — For its magnetic qualities. **Alabaster** — Translucent material which softens the effect of light; traditionally employed for lamps and as window panes. **Rock crystal** — Attributed here as representing the colourless purity of elemental Air; also because crystal is employed in clairvoance to transmit psychic impressions and images.

12. **Opal** — The traditional gemstone of Mercury for its changeful and gleaming colours, also because opal is, by whatever

imperceptible degrees, evanescent: the substance of the stone consumes away in process of time. **Hyacinth (Jacinth)** — A variety of zircon, attributed to Mercury on account of its orange colour. **Tourmaline** — Appropriate to Mercury because it is a complex compound of aluminium, because of its variety of possible colours, and not least because of its curious electrical properties.

13. **Hyalite** — A colourless but luminescent variety of opal

14. **Rose Jade** — An exquisite symbol of the purity and beneficence of Celestial Venus as *Rosa mundi*. **Amber** — A natural, sea-borne emblem of Venus Anadyomene.

15. **Marcasite** — A crystallised and jewel-like form of iron pyrites. **Red jasper** — An opaque quartz combined and stained with iron oxide. Both the foregoing stones are symbols of Mars, ruling planet of the Sign Aries. **Spiral crystals** — An unusual formation, chosen as representing the horns of the Ram.

16. **Carnelian** — Frequently given to Mercury on account of its colour, which can be approximated to orange. The dense texture of the stone however gives it an affinity with Taurus, while its warm colour resembling flesh, from which the stone derives its name, associates it with Venus the ruling planet of Taurus. **Green jasper** — An opaque quartz whose green pigment relates it symbolically to Venus, while its opacity suits it to Taurus as a Sign of the earthy triplicity. **Steatite** — Also an opaque stone, steatite occurs in various neutral colours: its Venusian quality consists in the artistry with which it can be worked. Both green jasper and steatite were prevalent in the craftsmanship of the notably taurean Minoan culture.

17. **Iceland spar** — A transparent crystalline compound of calcium, which refracts a double image of any object which is perceived through it. **Shell cameos** — Distinguished by their naturally stratified colours, and by the expertise — a quality of Mercury, ruling planet of this Sign Gemini — shown in their fashioning.

18. **Selenium** — For its distinctive electrical sensitivity, which rises or falls according to the amount of illumination present; also for its name, which likewise relates to the Moon (*Selene*), ruling planet of the sign Cancer. **Crafted scarabs** — For the arising of Khepera from the primal watery abyss, and for the aspect of the sacred scarabaeus as zodiacal Cancer.

19. **Chatoyant stones. Yellow topaz, Yellow beryl** — All suggestive of the eyes of lions and of other felines.

20. **Green jade, white jade** — Emblems of purity in Chinese traditions. **Feldspar** — Mainly aluminium silicate. Appropriate to Virgo for its white or pale rose colour, and to the ruling planet Mercury because it is a compound of aluminium.

21. **Amethyst, lapis lazuli, bluejohn, labradorite** — All these stones are symbolic of the celestial governance of Jupiter. Labradorite is an opaque, lustrous stone resembling turquoise but of a more intense and dominant colour.

22. **Rose pearl, banded malachite** — Both these stones are representative of Venus, the ruling planet of Libra: the first for tender beauty, the second as a major symbol of Netzach; but both also typify the Sign Libra, the rose pearl representing peace and serenity, the banded malachite an equilibrium of shades of green

23. **Aquamarine, pale green beryl, white pearl, mother-of-pearl** — All these stones are especially representative of elemental Water.

24. **Obsidian** — A volcanic glass, translucent and of very dark green colour. **Bloodstone** — A dark green stone with spots of red. **Serpentine** — A dark green stone capable of a high lustre, and frequently dappled like the skin of a snake. All these stones relate to the letter Nun and to the Sign Scorpio, the influence upon this Path.

25. **Blue turquoise** — Traditional stone of Sagittarius and of the skyey aspect of its ruler Jupiter. **Deep violet amethyst** — For the zenith of the heavens. **Golden topaz, Zircon** — emblematic of the high solar aspirations of this Path.

26. **Smoky topaz, black opal** — For the Sign Capricorn which is represented upon this Path, and its ruling planet Saturn. **Concentric stones** — Most often onyx, agate or quartz. The concentric banding suggests an eye, for the letter Ayin.

27. **Meteoric rock** — For its fiery descent. **Volcanic rock** — As corresponding to Mars, but also with reference to the letter of the Path: Peh, "the Mouth".

28. **Geodes. Blister pearls** — Naturally hollow mineral structures, given here in allusion to the pitcher of air-sign Aquarius. **Amber with winged inclusions** — Another interpretation, this time of a symbol of air enclosed in a mineral casing.

29. **Baroque pearls** — Without the status of regularly shaped pearls, these interesting sea-gems often have somewhat the forms of fish. **Pale sapphire** — This stone has much, both in pallor and in brilliance, of the character of water and of its gleaming denizens. **Amethyst matrix** — Celebrates Jupiter as the ruling planet of Pisces, but in a mode which is less assertive than that of the true gemstone, and at the same time is more suggestive of the watery ambience of this Path.

30. **Hyacinth (jacinth), yellow or golden topaz, crysoleth** — Upon this Path these glorious stones simply represent the Sun.

31. **Flint** — A potently operative symbol of Fire: not only igneous in its origin, but itself productive of living flame when employed with steel.

32. **Black marble, onyx** — For Binah-Saturn.

BIBLIOGRAPHY

ABRAI, James, *Christian Mysteries in the Light of Jungian Psychology: St. John of the Cross and Dr. C.G. Jung,* Chiloquin, U.S.A., 1986.
AUGUSTINE, St. (Aurelius Augustinus), *De natura boni,* Migne, Patrologia Latina vol. 42, cols. 551-572.
De natura boni. Included in <u>The Earlier Writings of St. Augustine</u>, selected and translated by John H.S. Burleigh, Library of Christian Classics No. 6, London 1953.
Liber de Spiritu et Anima, Migne, Patr. Lat. vol. 40, cols. 779-832.
In Ioannis Evangelium, tractatus CXXIV, Migne, Patr. Lat. vol. 35, cols. 1379-1976.
Tractatus in Ioannis Evangelium, translated by James Innes. *Works of Aurelius Augustinus,* edited by Marcus Dodds. (2 vols.), Edinburgh 1874.
Ad inquisitiones Januarii liber primus, seu Epistola LIV: liber secundus, seu Epistola LV, Migne, Patr. Lat. vol. 33, cols. 200-223.
The Letters of St. Augustine. Edited by W. Sparrow-Simpson, London 1919, (for Letters to Januarius)
Quaestiones in Exodum, Migne, Patr. Lat. vol. 34, cols. 597-657.
Sermonis VIII, De decem plagis et decem praeceptis, Migne, Patr. Lat. vol. 38 cols. 67-74.
De Trinitate, Migne, Patr. Lat. vol. 42, cols. 819-1098.
BENSION, Ariel, *El Zohar en la España Musulmana y Cristiana,* Madrid 1931.

BERTHELOT, M, *Collection des anciens alchimistes grecs (3 vols.),* Paris 1887-88.

CHARLES, R.H, *Apocrypha and Pseudepigraphia of the Old Testament (2 vols.),* Oxford 1913, (In particular for The Book of Enoch, which contains much traditional angelology.)

CICERO, *De natura deorum. Concerning the Nature of the Gods.* Latin text with English translation by H. Rackham, Loeb Classical Library, London/New York 1933.

COPLESTON, Frederick, SJ, *A History of Philosophy. Volume I, Greece and Rome* (in which Part V, Post-Aristotelian Philosophy, contains a chapter on Jewish-Hellenistic philosophy). *Volume II, Mediaeval Philosophy* (in which Part IV treats of Islamic and Jewish philosophy, and of mediaeval traditions), Burns & Oates, 1966.

CORTE, Marcel de, *Plotin et la "Nuit de l'esprit",* Etudes Carmélitaines 23, pp. 1012-1015, 1938.

CROWLEY, Aleister, *Magick in Theory and Practice,* Dover, New York, 1976.

CUMONT, Franz, *The Mysteries of Mithra,* Dover Books, U.S.A., 1966.

DENNING, M & PHILLIPS, O, *The Magical Philosophy. (5 vols),* Llewellyn, U.S.A., 1974-1979; 3 vols. revised enlarged edn., Llewellyn 1986-1991.

DIONYSIUS the Areopagite (pseud.), *Liber tertius: De divinis nominibus,* Migne, Patr. Lat. vol. 122, cols. 1113-1172.

FICINO, Marsilio, *Opera. (2 vols.),* Basle 1576.
De vita libri tres, Basle 1549.
Liber de vita, the Book of Life. Translated by Charles Boer. Spring Books, U.S.A, 1980.
Marsile Ficin. Commentaire sur le Banquet de Platon: texte du manuscrit autographe présenté et traduit par Raymond Marcel, attaché de recherches au Centre National de la Recherche Scientifique, Soc. d'Edition "Les Belles Lettres", Paris 1956.
The Letters of Marsilio Ficino, translated by members of the Language Department, School of Economic Science, London, Shepheard-Walwyn, London 1975-1988.
(See also **RANDOLPH, Paschal Beverly**)

FORTUNE, Dion, *The Mystical Qabalah,* Ernest Benn, London 1957

GABIROL, Solomon ibn (also called **AVICEBRON**), *Avencebrolis Fons Vitae, ex arabico in latinum translatus ab Ioanno Hispano et Dominico Gundissalino,* Münster 1892-95. (See also **MYERS, Isaac**)

GODWIN, David, *Godwin's Cabalistic Encyclopedia: A Complete Guide to Cabalistic Magic,* Llewellyn, U.S.A., 1989.

GRAVES, Robert, *The Greek Myths (2 vols.),* Penguin, Harmondsworth. Revised 1957

GREENBERG, Rabbi Morris, *One Place. Selected readings from the Book of Splendour,* translated from the Aramaic and collated with various Hebrew and Latin commentaries, Unpublished MS. in the collection of the authors. 1929.

The Hands of the Holy One: Meditations on the Shield of David for the Day of Atonement, Unpublished MS. in the collection of the authors. 1932.

HOLY SCRIPTURES *according to the Masoretic Text (2 vols.)* Jewish Publication Society of America, Philadelphia 1955.

JAMES, E.O, *Myth and Ritual in the Ancient Near East,* Thames & Hudson, 1958.

JOHN OF THE CROSS (St.), *San Juan de la Cruz: Obras Completas,* Editorial de Espiritualidad, Madrid 1992.

Dark Night of the Soul, by St. John of the Cross. Translated by E. Allison Peers. 3rd revised edition (1953) from the critical Spanish edition of P. Silverio de Santa Teresa, CD. With translator's preface and introduction, Burns & Oates 1935, revised 1953, new edition 1976.

Living Flame of Love, by St. John of the Cross. Translated by E. Allison Peers from the critical edition of P. Silverio de Santa Teresa, CD. With translator's introduction, Burns & Oates 1935, new edition 1977.

JUNG, C.G, *The Structure and Dynamics of the Psyche,* Routledge & Kegan Paul, revised edition 1969.

The Archetypes and the Collective Unconscious, Routledge & Kegan Paul, 1959.

Psychology and Alchemy, Routledge & Kegan Paul, 1953. 2nd edn. completely revised, 1958.

Alchemical Studies, Routledge & Kegan Paul, 1967.
KIRCHER, Athanasius, *Cabala Hebraeorum,* Rome 1652.
KNORR VON ROSENROTH, Christian, *Kabbala Denudata. (2 vols.),* Sulzbach & Frankfurt-a-M, 1677-1684.
(See also MATHERS, S.L. MacGregor)
MARDON-ROBINSON, E, *La nuit de l'esprit selon Jean de la Croix et ses rapports avec la mélancholie,* In "Mémoire et psychiatrie", Marseilles 1982.
MATHERS, S.L. MacGregor, *Kabbalah Denudata: The Kabbalah Unveiled. Containing the following books of the Zohar: 1. The Book of Concealed Mystery. 2. The Greater Holy Assembly. 3. The Lesser Holy Assembly.* Translated ... from the Latin of Knorr von Rosenroth, and collated with the original Chaldee and Hebrew text by S.L. MacGregor Mathers, G. Redway, London 1887.
Kabbalah Denudata: The Kabbalah Unveiled, 4th impression, Kegan Paul, London 1926. Reprinted 1976.
MEAD, G.R.S, *The Doctrine of the Subtle Body in Western Tradition,* London 1919.
(See PISTIS SOPHIA)
MEUNIER, Mario, *Hymnes philosophiques: Aristote, Cléanthe, Proclus.* French translation from the Greek, with notes, L'Artisan du Livre, Paris 1935.
MOORE, Thomas, *The Planets Within,* Associated University Presses, London & Toronto, 1982.
MYERS, Isaac
Qabbalah. The Philosophical Writings of Solomon ibn Gebirol or Avicebron and their connection with the Hebrew Qabbalah and Sepher ha-Zohar, with ... translation of selected passages from the same. (Published by the author, Philadelphia 1888)
OVID , *Metamorphoses.* Latin text with English translation by F.J. Miller (2 vols.) (Loeb Classical Library 1946)
PARROT, André, *The Flood and Noah's Ark.* (Originally published in French by Delachaux & Niestlé, Neuchatel 1953: English version publ. by SCM Press, London 1955)
The Tower of Babel. (Originally published in French by Delachaux & Niestlé, Neuchatel 1954: English version publ. by SCM Press, London 1955)

Bibliography 169

PICO della MIRANDOLA, Giovanni, *Heptaplus. Included in Opera* (Venice 1557) and *"Opera omnia"* (Basle 1572-73) *De Hominis Dignitate — Heptaplus — De Ente et Uno. E scritti vari a cura di Eugenio Garin* (Latin texts with Italian translation) (Vallecchi Editore, Firenze 1942)

PISTIS SOPHIA, (Anon.) Translated into English by G.R.S. Mead. (University Books, U.S.A., 1974)

PLATO, *The Symposium,* translated and edited by R.G. Bury. (Cambridge 1909)
The Symposium, translated by W. Hamilton (Penguin, Harmondsworth)

PHILO of Alexandria, *De Opificio Mundi. On the account of the World's Creation given by Moses.* (Loeb Classical Library, Vol. 1 of the Works of Philo, 1929)

RANDOLPH, Paschal Beverly (Editor), *Hermes Mercurius Trismegistus, his Divine Pymander (etc.)* The Pymander is given in the translation of Dr. Everard (first publ. 1650) from the Latin version of Marsilio Ficino (first published 1471) (Rosicrucian Publishing Co., 1871; Randolph Publishing Co., Toledo, Ohio, U.S.A. 1889)

REUCHLIN, Johann, *De arte cabalistica.* (Hagenau 1517)
La Kabbale. French translation by François Secret of Reuchlin's De arte cabalistica. (Aubier-Montaigne, Paris 1973)

ROUGIER, Louis, *La Religion astrale des Pythagoriciens.* (Presses Universitaires, Paris 1959)

SCHOLEM, Gershom, *Alchemie und Kabbala.* Ein Kapitel aus der Geschichte der Mystik (Berlin 1927)
Bibliographia Kabbalistica. Verzeichnis der gedruckten die jüdische Mystik ... Mit einem Anhang: Bibliographie des Zohar under seiner Kommentare. (Leipzig 1927)
Einige kabbalistische Handschriften im Britischen Museum. (Vorabdruck aus: Soncino-Blätter, Beiträge zur Kunde des judischen Buches.) (Jerusalem/Berlin: printed 1932)
Les grands courants de la mystique juive. (Payot, Paris 1968)
Zohar, the Book of Splendor: Basic readings from the Kabbalah (Schocken Books, New York 1953)
Zur Kabbala und ihrer Symbolik (Rhein-Verlag, Zurich 1960) On the Kabbalah and its symbolism (The above, translated by Ralph Manheim) (Schocken Books, New York 1969)

SCOTT, Walter, *Hermetica — Corpus Hermeticum* — the ancient Greek and Latin writings which contain religious & philosophical teachings ascribed to Hermes Trismegistus. (4 vols.) Vol. 1: Introduction, Texts and Translation. (Shambhala, Boston, U.S.A., 1985)

SMITH, Sir William, and FULLER, Revd. J.M. *A Dictionary of the Bible* (3 vols. in 4 books) (John Murray, London 1893)

WAITE, A.E. *The Doctrine and Literature of the Kabbalah.* (Theosophical Publishing Co., London 1902)
The Holy Kabbalah: a study of the secret tradition in Israel. (Williams & Newgate, London 1929)
The Secret Doctrine in Israel: a study of the Zohar and its connections. (William Rider & Son, London 1913)

ZOHAR, The. English translation by Harry Sperling, Maurice Simon and Dr. Paul P. Levertoff. With Introduction by Dr. J. Abelson. (5 vols.) (Soncino Press, London 1931-34)
Sepher ha-Zohar, le Livre de la Splendeur: doctrine ésotérique des Israélites. Traduit pour le premier fois sur le texte chaldaique et accompagné des notes par Jean de Pauly. Oeuvre posthume entièrement revue, corrigée et completée, publiée par les soins d'Emile Lafuma-Giraud (Paris 1911)
Traduction intégrale du Siphra di-Tzeniutha, le livre secret, oeuvrage essentiel du Sepher ha-Zohar II, fol. 176b-179a. Comprenant deux versions, l'une littérale l'autre paraphrasée, avec notes critiques et commentaires initiatiques; augmentée d'une préface ... et de nouvelles considérations sur l'antiquité du Zohar. Edité et traduit par Paul Villiaud. (Paris 1930)

Other titles from Thoth Publications

AN INTRODUCTION TO RITUAL MAGIC
By Dion Fortune & Gareth Knight

At the time this was something of a unique event in esoteric publishing - a new book by the legendary Dion Fortune. Especially with its teachings on the theory and practice of ritual or ceremonial magic, by one who, like the heroine of two of her other novels, was undoubtedly "a mistress of that art".

In this work Dion Fortune deals in successive chapters with Types of Mind Working; Mind Training; The Use of Ritual; Psychic Perception; Ritual Initiation; The Reality of the Subtle Planes; Focusing the Magic Mirror; Channelling the Forces; The Form of the Ceremony; and The Purpose of Magic - with appendices on Talisman Magic and Astral Forms.

Each chapter is supplemented and expanded by a companion chapter on the same subject by Gareth Knight. In Dion Fortune's day the conventions of occult secrecy prevented her from being too explicit on the practical details of magic, except in works of fiction. These veils of secrecy having now been drawn back, Gareth Knight has taken the opportunity to fill in much practical information that Dion Fortune might well have included had she been writing today.

In short, in this unique collaboration of two magical practitioners and teachers, we are presented with a valuable and up-to-date text on the practice of ritual or ceremonial magic "as it is". 'That is to say, as a practical, spiritual, and psychic discipline, far removed from the lurid superstition and speculation that are the hall mark of its treatment in sensational journalism and channels of popular entertainment.

ISBN 1-870450 31 0 Deluxe Hardback Limited edition
ISBN 1-870450 26 4 Soft cover edition

THE CIRCUIT OF FORCE
by Dion Fortune.
With commentaries by Gareth Knight.

In "The Circuit of Force", Dion Fortune describes techniques for raising the personal magnetic forces within the human aura and their control and direction in magic and in life, which she regards as 'the Lost Secrets of the Western Esoteric Tradition'.

To recover these secrets she turns to three sources.

a) the Eastern Traditions of Hatha Yoga and Tantra and their teaching on raising the "sleeping serpent power" or kundalini;

b) the circle working by means of which spiritualist seances concentrate power for the manifestation of some of their results;

c) the linking up of cosmic and earth energies by means of the structured symbol patterns of the Qabalistic Tree of Life.

Originally produced for the instruction of members of her group, this is the first time that this material has been published for the general public in volume form.

Gareth Knight provides subject commentaries on various aspects of the etheric vehicle, filling in some of the practical details and implications that she left unsaid in the more secretive esoteric climate of the times in which she wrote.

Some quotes from Dion Fortune's text:

"When, in order to concentrate exclusively on God, we cut ourselves off from nature, we destroy our own roots. There must be in us a circuit between heaven and earth, not a one-way flow, draining us of all vitality. It is not enough that we draw up the Kundalini from the base of the spine; we must also draw down the divine light through the Thousand-Petalled Lotus. Equally, it is not enough for out mental health and spiritual development that we draw down the Divine Light, we must also draw up the earth forces. Only too often mental health is sacrificed to spiritual development through ignorance of, or denial of, this fact."

"....the clue to all these Mysteries is to be sought in the Tree of Life. Understand the significance of the Tree; arrange the symbols you are working with in the correct manner upon it, and all is clear and you can work out your sum. Equate the Danda with the Central Pillar, and the Lotuses with the Sephiroth and the bi-sections of the Paths thereon, and you have the necessary bilingual dictionary at your disposal - if you known how to use it."

ISBN 1-870450 23 X Deluxe Hardback Limited edition
ISBN 1-870450 28 0 Soft cover edition

THE SHINING PATHS
by Dolores Ashcroft-Nowicki

An Experiential Journey through the Tree of Life.

A unique collection of magical pathworkings based on the thirty-two paths of the Qabalistic Tree of Life.

Since it was first published The Shining Paths has become a classic of its kind, and an invaluable aid for both students and teachers.

Pathworking is the old name for what are now known as Guided Meditations. They are specifically designed visualisations into which the mind-self is projected into an inner world of learning events and situations which with training can become a complete sensory experience.

Dolores Ashcroft-Nowicki is one of the best known and most respected of contemporary Western occultists. In this book she offers a unique collection of pathworkings based on the Qabalistic Tree of Life. Each working is preceded by a discussion on the correspondences experiences, and symbology of that path.

Dolores Ashcroft-Nowicki is a third generation psychic sensitive and a symbiotic channeller, who has worked with magic since childhood. A student of the late W.E.Butler, she was one of the Founders of The Servants of the Light School of Occult Science, of which she is now the Director of Studies. She travels the world extensively lecturing and teaching on all aspects of occultism, bringing to her students the accumulated knowledge of over half a century of study and practice.

ISBN 1-870450-30-2

PRACTICAL MAGIC IN THE NORTHERN TRADITION

by Nigel Pennick

The Northern Tradition is the indigenous spiritual and magical system of European peoples north of the Alps. With its origin in archaic shamanic nature-veneration, it embodies the observances, practices and tradition of the people of the Celtic, Germanic, Scandinavian and Baltic realms. Practical Magic in the Northern Tradition cuts through the meaningless barriers between people, for these traditions and practices are linked with one another at the deepest level through common themes. The underlying magical principles are identical, being relevant to the same set of environmental conditions.

Many Northern Tradition observances have continued unbroken to the present day as folk customs, rural practices, household magic and the veneration of saints. Now, the Northern Tradition has emerged again in its own right, in a form appropriate for these times. This book is the definitive work of the tradition.

When we view the world in this way, Nature, personified as goddesses, gods and spirits, becomes approachable. It is all too apparent that the materialist ways of modernity can lead only to the destruction of Nature. The Northern Tradition provides another way, one of harmony with the natural world. Northern Tradition magic gives us the tools to bring ourselves into a dynamic interaction with the cyclic workings of Nature. By following the age-old festival customs described in this book, we can become attuned to the natural cycle of the seasons and harmonise ourselves with Nature and our fellow human beings.

ISBN 1-870450-16-7

PRACTICAL MAGIC AND THE WESTERN MYSTERY TRADITION

Unpublished Essays and Articles by W. E. Butler.

W. E. Butler, a devoted friend and colleague of the celebrated occultist Dion Fortune, was among those who helped build the Society of the Inner Light into the foremost Mystery School of its day. He then went on to found his own school, the Servants of the Light, which still continues under the guidance of Dolores Ashcroft-Nowicki, herself an occultist and author of note and the editor and compiler of this volume.

PRACTICAL MAGIC AND THE WESTERN MYSTERY TRADITION is a collection of previously unpublished articles, training papers, and lectures covering many aspects of practical magic in the context of western occultism that show W. E. Butler not only as a leading figure in the magical tradition of the West, but also as one of its greatest teachers.

Subjects covered include:

What makes an occultist
Ritual training
Inner Plane contacts and Rays
The Witch Cult
Keys in Practical Magic
Telesmatic images
Words of Power
An Explanation of Some Psychic Phenomena

ISBN 1-870450 32-9

THE PATH THROUGH THE LABYRINTYH
by Marian Green

The Quest for Initiation into the Western Mystery Tradition.

Underlying the evolving culture of the West there hides a complete strata of folk-lore, of traditional skills and wisdom, of ancient arts and festivals.

These are still emerging in myth and legend, in song and celebrations, each retaining aspects of a very great initiatory system rooted in the land and its magic.

Most available sources tell the reader about the how to of magic, but for the first time this book explores the way of magic, and the what happens when... of modern magical techniques.

In The Path Through the Labyrinth, Marian Green, a highly respected practitioner and teacher of the Western Tradition, examines these questions and guides the reader safely to the heart of the magical maze, and then out again.

ISBN 1-870450-15-9

*   *   *   *   *

PRACTICAL TECHNIQUES OF MODERN MAGIC
by Marian Green

> What is the essence of ritual magic?
> How are the symbols used to create change?
> Can I safely take steps in ritual on my own?
> How does magic fit into the pattern of life in the modern world?
> Will I be able to master the basic arts?
> All these questions and many more are answered within the pages of this book.

ISBN 1-870450-14-0